3 Plays

BY

Henry Kitt

A Moment in Orbit
Move and Counter-Move
What Do You Mean By That?

Capricornis Press
New York

Library of Congress Catalog Card Number: 91-71252
ISBN 0-924694-14-9
Printed in the United States of America

About the Author

Born March 2, 1912 in Baltimore, Maryland the late Henry Kitt was the fourth child of six.

After graduation from Teacher's College in Towson, Maryland and six months of teaching, he decided to travel cross-country to expand his experiences and enrich his mind.

He settled in New York and attended John Gassner's class in playwriting at the New School for Social Research. He was offered a contract with Columbia Pictures but rejected it to continue writing for the theater.

In addition to his many plays, he has written two volumes of essays in Social Philosophy: "A Passionate Love of Mankind" Kitt's Law – The PLOM Theory, Vol. 1, Vol. 2.

A fatal heart-attack on April 26, 1985 ended his life.

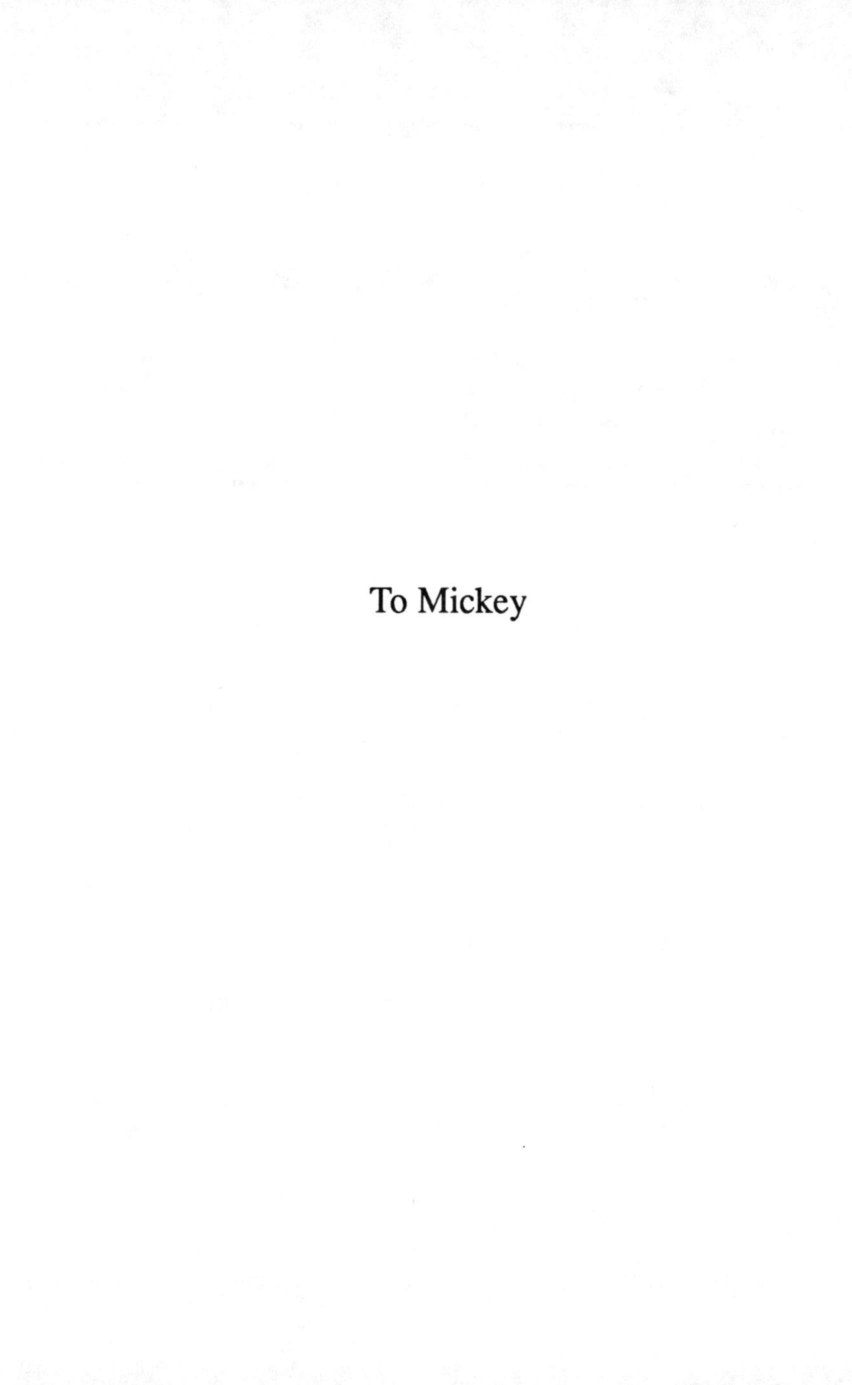

To Mickey

3 Plays

A Moment In Orbit

CHARACTERS

DANIEL HOFFMAN
FLORENCE
AL
FRED
ANNIE

A Moment In Orbit

A poorly lit, frayed and mangy-looking drugstore in a downtown area of Manhattan. It is a small place, and along the back there is a glass-doored case topped by a worn linoleum counter which supports a cash register and the usual low-priced items. An open doorway to the back room is right of the counter; below the doorway a telephone booth. Two round wooden chairs project at right angles to the counter.

Behind the counter is DANIEL HOFFMAN, middle-aged, carelessly dressed with no concern for fashion, and possessing a strange air of ease and timelessness.

At curtain, he is drinking a cup of coffee; after the leisurely last sip, he places it on the shelf behind him. Now from the inside coat pocket of his jacket he lifts a bulky loose-leaf black plastic-covered notebook and makes an entry there.

A middle-aged woman enters.

DANIEL: *[Casually replacing the book into his pocket.]* Annie, you look to me as if you're looking for something.
ANNIE: Last night — I didn't sleep too good last night. Tossed all the night. . . . My throat's dry . . . all day. . .
DANIEL: Scratchy?
ANNIE: Like, feels . . . yeah — dry. . . .
DANIEL: Eyes feel tight?

ANNIE: Yeah, and burning. I didn't sleep so hot. They burn . . .

DANIEL: Ahh, the classic symptoms, Annie. You're just coming down with a little cold. Scratchy throat, you're eyes. We'll nip it in the bud before it gets a hold. Here — *[Picking up a small box from the counter.]* . . . take these APC's four times a day. Along with this — *[Hauling up a bottle from a drawer.]* One teaspoon of this Histadyl and codeine also four times a day. You can take them at the same time. That'll knock it right into kingdom come.

ANNIE: *[Holding up the box.]* Two of these. . . ?

DANIEL: Two of these tablets four times a day. And one teaspoon of this four times a day. Take them both, like black beans in a soup — both together. And go to bed early. Get plenty of sleep. A lot of sleep. You get yourself plenty of sleep.

ANNIE: Four times a day . . .

DANIEL: Two APC's four times a day . . .

ANNIE: *[Again showing the box.]* Four times a day . . .

DANIEL: Four times a day: also, one teaspoon. In other words, four times a day — this and this.

ANNIE: Two of these pills four times a day, and one teaspoon of this cough medicine four times . . .

DANIEL: No — that's not cough medicine. What we call a preventive, Annie — kicks a cold in the nose so you won't get a cough.

ANNIE: How much?

DANIEL: All told, a mighty — fifteen, seventy-five — a big ninety cents. You kill a dollar but you get back change. *[ANNIE digs up a dollar from her purse.]* How's that plaguy burn on your leg?

ANNIE: All gone — wonderful. Completely healed up.

DANIEL: Good. Good. Good. Good.
ANNIE: Only a couple times I used it. Altogether, three times — the salve you give me.
DANIEL: Anytime you burn yourself use it. One of my special formulas.
ANNIE: Healed it up like magic. *[He gives her change. The phone rings.]*
DANIEL: Take both of those four times a day. Go to bed as soon as you can. Plenty of sleep — sleep. *[He turns toward the phone, dismissing her totally as he does so ANNIE waddles off; DANIEL takes the phone.]* Orbit Pharmacy . . . Hello . . . How is Berny Flinn? . . . So what happened? . . . Ahah . . . Ahah . . . Ahah . . . All right, come in tomorrow; I'll double the strength of the lead acetate and the acacia. I'll have you looking ten years younger — fifteen . . . Nobody can tell it's not your own natural color . . . Why not? On the ear — I can take care of — a little two percent solution of silver nitrate. No problem — no problem at all . . . Sure, nobody wants to hire a gray-haired sales clerk. You have to give your business age, instead of your calendar age. It's your business age . . . *[Aware of someone coming into the store.]* I'm busy now, Barny. Come in tomorrow. I'll fix you up perfect with the double strength. *[He hangs up, and advances briskly toward the counter. A stoutish, well-dressed woman is being helped into the store by a stoutish, florid-faced man.]*
FRED: She hurt herself . . . somebody —
DANIEL: What happened? What's the trouble?
FLORENCE: *[In great pain.]* May I sit down, please? *[Daniel carefully helps her to one of the two wooden chairs.]*
FLORENCE: *[Sitting down.]* Thank you. . . .
DANIEL: What's the trouble?
FRED: She fell down . . . I helped her up —

DANIEL: *[Very concerned.]* Fall down?

FLORENCE: *[Rubbing the instep of her left foot.]* I twisted my foot. . . .

FRED: I figured, Doc, she'd be better off . . .

DANIEL: Of course . . .

FLORENCE: This boy . . . on a bicycle . . . ran into me . . . Ooooh-h . . . Without so much as an excuse to me, he ran off . . .

FRED: The kids around here, Mam, they're a bunch 'a ferocious monkeys.

DANIEL: Is that . . . the only reason . . . you fell down?

FRED: No more manners than a bunch 'a wild baboons.

DANIEL: *[Pointing to her foot.]* Let me see there . . .

FLORENCE: *[Intensely worried.]* I have this appointment, uptown . . .

DANIEL: Devil the appointment. You feel all right?

FLORENCE: I wonder — Could I call a cab?

DANIEL: We'll get you a cab, in due time.

FLORENCE: I must get uptown.

DANIEL: Uptown and all can wait. That's not essential right now. *[She peers at him.]* Believe me. Whatever is uptown can wait. It'll be there later, I assure you.

FLORENCE: I have an appointment with a doctor.

DANIEL: Ahah. Why?

FLORENCE: *[Affronted.]* Isn't that . . .

FRED: Keep them doctors waiting one second. You hang around their office for hours — scratching your ears for hours — but just you miss by a minute when they're ready —

FLORENCE: *[Pointedly.]* Please wait on your customer. *[Looking toward the phone booth.]* I'll be all right. Thank you very much.

FRED: No hurry here, Mam. I'm glad that's just a bump. I mean, so many people with heart attacks smacking the pavements all over the city. You see it every day.

DANIEL: In a drug store you see it all. As long as it's nothing more than your foot?

FLORENCE: Nothing — it was the pain . . .

DANIEL: I'll take care of that in a minute. Soon as I fix up the gentleman.

FRED: *[Handing him a prescription.]* Just this, Doc . . .

[FLORENCE glances again at the phone booth then makes a test of her foot. Suddenly, she winces.]

DANIEL: *[Reading the prescription.]* What happened to that fifty I just —

FRED: I'm takin' 'em ten times a day, Doc. They don't last —

DANIEL: Ten? That bad?

FRED: Oh, boy-y . . . *[Tapping the left side of his chest.]* Shoohhhh . . .

DANIEL: How long's that been going on?

FRED: Ah-h, couple years . . .

DANIEL: *[Shaking his head.]* Ten a day . . . One one-hundredth . . .

FRED: When these pains come on — I'd take anything . . .

DANIEL: What kind of work do you do?

FRED: Construction. I'm a construction worker.

DANIEL: You ought to take off a little weight.

FRED: Yeah-h. My doctor there's been harping the same thing.

DANIEL: He's right. How much sleep do you get?

FRED: You kiddin'? Sleep? If I get two hours a night — I don't remember what sleep is.

DANIEL: You can't go on like this.

FRED: Tops — two hours. Jeez, sleep. . . .

DANIEL: Why doesn't your doctor give you a sleeping remedy?

FRED: He says I'm gettin' my rest in bed. He doesn't want me to get in the habit. . . .

DANIEL: Nonsense. That's plain barbarian nonsense.

FRED: My doctor said —

DANIEL: I know. Look if you don't sleep, you don't rest. This joke — idiotic nonsense. Besides you're taking too much nitroglycerin here. That's too much, one one-hundredth grains. And no sleep. You go get yourself some nembutal, a half grain. . . .

FRED: My doctor won't give me none of that. . . ..

DANIEL: So what? *[FLORENCE looks up at him sharply.]*

FRED: It's dope, that stuff. You get nailed in the habit. That's one thing on top of everything I don't want.

DANIEL: I'll tell you what I call that — normalosis nonsense. People don't get in the habit. Not if you use it wisely, therapeutically. I know people who have been using it on and off for thirty years. Myself — I've been taking it myself at least twenty. Don't let the doctors frighten you. This dope business is just a boogey-man — infantile. You have to sleep, mister. How long you gonna kibitz this pain in your chest? That's angina pectoris. You can't play around with two hours sleep a night. You're inviting murder — handing it a silver invitation every minute. You've got to get a good night's sleep, every night. At least eight hours a night. Eight hours *sleep — not* tossing in bed.

FRED: Yeah, but my doctor won't give me no prescription —

DANIEL: You go across the street here, right across the street to Dr. DeMartino. Tell him your trouble. He'll give it to you. You've got to sleep, Mr. Ferris. Sleep is the great natural healer. That'll do you as much good — more good, believe me. Number two, I'm going to cut the dose down for you to one four-hundredth of nitroglycerine.

FRED: *[Protesting with the deepest anxiety.]* Look, uh . . ! — These pains —

DANIEL: Give it a test, try out a test, Mr. Ferris.

FRED: I better not. If you —

DANIEL: Just make a trial. See what happens. Do a little self-research. If these one four-hundredths don't give you as much relief as your one one-hundredths — go back on your one one-hundredths. You can always go back. Besides, the one four-hundredths I'm asking you to try won't give you any headaches . . .

FRED: *[Surprised.]* You mean . . . all these headaches . . . ?

DANIEL: Certainly — there's the cause. Didn't your doctor tell you? This nitroglycerine dilates the blood vessels — that's what happens. So in the brain — they press against the brain. You won't get any headaches with one four-hundredth . . . there's a little less swelling — makes a difference. . . *[Takes a bottle from the back shelf.]* I'll give you ten. You can test it out. *[He pours ten tablets into a box, then writes the name of the drug and its strength on the label. FLORENCE all this while has been staring at him, shaking her head in marked criticism and disbelief.]* Right. *[Pulling out a cheap watch from his trouser watch pocket.]* Dr. DeMartino'll be in at 5:30. You go across and get him to give you a barbiturate — Nembutal, Seconal. Then come back here. I'm gonna fix you up, I'm gonna make you feel life's worth living.

FRED: Yeah, you wonder. Tossin' nights — thinkin' . . .

DANIEL: The easiest, quickest, best-guaranteed way to get yourself shoved under the green sod.

FRED: You ain't kiddin' one bit, Doc. Awww —

DANIEL: We have to take care of the lady now. You can pay me after — when you get back from Dr. DeMartino's. Meantime, I'll fill your doctor's prescription.

FRED: Thanks, Doc. Thanks. I didn't connect those headaches . . . *[To FLORENCE.]* Without sleep it's a botch — Doc's a hundred percent right. A hundred percent.

[FLORENCE smiles stiffly. FRED goes off.]

DANIEL: Let's see that foot now.

FLORENCE: *[Jerking it away from him.]* It'll be all right.

DANIEL: That's swollen. You must have twisted it badly.

FLORENCE: *[Trying to stand up.]* I'll. . . .

DANIEL: Why don't you let me make you a cold compress there. It'll be black and blue tomorrow.

FLORENCE: Thank you. I'll take care of it. May I use your phone to call my doctor?

DANIEL: It's a public phone. *[The phone rings.]* Let me get this. You'll be right next. *[He crosses to the phone booth and takes phone.]* Orbit Pharmacy . . . Yes, this is Daniel . . . What's the trouble, Elizabeth? . . . Sure, that's life . . . But don't you remember the poem . . . "This minute if I smile at once, The sun of hope begins to flow. . . " Now Elizabeth . . . You must stop this crying . . . the more you cry . . . Elizabeth . . . Elizabeth . . . Elizabeth, do you hear me? . . . I understand, Elizabeth, I understand. You know I understand . . . You've been coming to my class nearly a year. Have I told you anything that turned out wrong . . . Now I want you to — Elizabeth, make yourself two strong cups of tea right away. And take one aspirin and one APC.

Right away . . . I want you to hang up — that's right, no
more tears. Drink two cups of strong tea — with one APC
and one aspirin. And I want to see you here in an hour
. . . Now, Elizabeth. You've too much to live for to go on
like this. I've always believed in you. I'm asking you to do
this for yourself . . . for your self . . . Fine. Now you, you
make yourself, immediately, two strong cups of tea, and
remember —

   "This minute if I smile at once — *smile* at once,
   The sun of hope begins to flow . . ."
Fine. *Right away. [He hangs up, standing there a moment
worried. Then: more to himself.]* If she does what I told her.
She was in a bad way. Talked of committing suicide. One
of my students — I teach a class —
FLORENCE: Doesn't she have a psychiatrist?
DANIEL: I suppose she ought to . . . But I've helped a lot
of people by teaching them —
FLORENCE: *[Moving toward the phone — curtly.]* It seems
to me only a psychiatrist would be of any help — *[Again the
phone rings.]*
DANIEL: I better take this. I'll make it real quick. I don't
think it's anybody — *[FLORENCE is markedly disappointed.
She tries her foot as she looks out to the door. Daniel takes the
phone.]* Orbit . . . Yes . . . Who? . . . Oh, yes . . . Since when?
. . . Well, take some Kaopectate . . . Go to your drugstore
and get a bottle . . . Kaopectate, sure, that's it . . . Good, I'm
a little busy . . . *[He is about to hang up. FLORENCE has
started to limp out of the store, but turns when she hears him give
his caller both a medical diagnosis and medication via phone.]*
What. . . ? What's the matter with your dog? . . . Your dog,
huh? Let me hear . . . Pick him up: put his mouth to the
phone . . . Tell him to breath . . . Umhmmm . . . Mmmmm-

hmmmm. The poor pooch . . . I hear it. I hear it. That's a resonant bronchitic breathing for sure. All right, when you go out to get the Kaopectate for your diarrhea, buy a box of chocolate kisses. Give your dog one of the chocolate kisses every hour. One every hour . . . It's emollient — has a moistening fat . . . No, just one's enough. I'm busy with the store . . . Okay. *[He hangs up. To FLORENCE.]* Quick — better hurry. It's an afternoon . . .

FLORENCE: *[Puzzled.]* Are you . . . a physician?

DANIEL: Oh, no-o — no . . . Don't stand too much on that foot.

FLORENCE: Isn't it against the law to practice medicine unless you're a physician. I mean diagnosing illnesses, dispensing medications. . .

DANIEL: Such is the fate, the lot of a druggist. He's always acting outside the law.

FLORENCE: It doesn't seem to trouble you at all?

DANIEL: Can't be helped. Your apothecary since ancient days — all the way back —

FLORENCE: This is the most shocking — Changing doctors' prescriptions at will — prescribing narcotics — barbiturates, casually . . .

DANIEL: Oh, I'd hardly call —

FLORENCE: Numbutal, Seconal — those are habit-forming barbiturates. And only a physician has the right . . .

DANIEL: Only a physician? And habit-forming?

FLORENCE: Indeed! Indeed! Indeed they are!

DANIEL: They also happen to be wonderful remedies.

FLORENCE: Under a doctor's supervision. Yes. You are *not* a physician.

DANIEL: If used intelligently there's never —

FLORENCE: You should be the last person — in a position

of trust as you are. These are terrible habits . . .

DANIEL: Not so terrible, I don't think.

FLORENCE: *You* don't think!?

DANIEL: No, I don't. Why shouldn't people use them if they help? I have a great deal of faith in peoples' natural intelligence. So you'd better get off that foot, or you'll be needing —

FLORENCE: *[Standing hard, with Spartan defiance.]* It is a well-established medical fact that people abuse —

DANIEL: Don't let well-established facts mesmerize you. I happen to have over-turned a couple of very well-established medical facts in times past. But I'm worried about your foot. If you want to use the phone . . .

FLORENCE: Is this the way it is in New York? Do all pharmacists here behave this way?

DANIEL: I don't know. Aren't you from New York?

FLORENCE: Perhaps if I were, I wouldn't . . .

DANIEL: You're standing too hard on that foot. Why don't you let me take a cold compress —

FLORENCE: How do you know it's not broken? A muscle torn — or a bone misplaced? You're not a doctor. How dare you take peoples' lives . . . like this . . .

DANIEL: I've been doing it for years . . .

FLORENCE: In broad daylight . . .

DANIEL: If you had a broken bone, there, or a torn muscle, madam, you wouldn't be able to stand on that foot so solidly as you are. I can also tell you it's going to be black and blue and yellow too, from long experience.

FLORENCE: My physician will take care of that.

DANIEL: The best physician prevents complications.

FLORENCE: *Physician — yes.*

DANIEL: You seem to think I am anti-doctor?

FLORENCE: No, not *sub rosa* doctors. *[Pointing across the street.]* That doctor you sent that poor man to — with angina pectoris. An*gina* pectoris.

DANIEL: Dr. DeMartino? Why he's one of the finest anywhere. Ask any doctor in the city who knows him. Go to his hospital . . .

FLORENCE: You've always wanted to be a doctor, haven't you?

DANIEL: Me? . . . No-o . . .

FLORENCE: No?

DANIEL: No — never a doctor. Oh, there've been times . . . when I've faced some spoiled arrogant idiot . . .

FLORENCE: Of course. You know so much more.

DANIEL: On occasion. Sometimes. That foot —

FLORENCE: *[Standing harder.]* Yes, it's evident. And so you use your position here to correct and dispense medical practice. Doesn't it concern you that you may be killing people everyday? Doesn't that touch you at all?

DANIEL: I've never had a corpse in thirty-five years. Can most doctors say as much?

FLORENCE: *Tea* and *aspirin* for a woman, who by your own account —

DANIEL: Strong tea.

FLORENCE: Tea and aspirin!

DANIEL: Two cups of strong tea, madam. With one APC and one aspirin. Try it yourself when you feel depressed. You —

FLORENCE: I've seldom in my life felt more depressed than this moment.

DANIEL: If you'll wait half a minute I can brew some tea . . . *[He points to the back room.]*

FLORENCE: You call this a drugstore? *This.* It is the

dirtiest, shabbiest, most miserably kept excuse for a drugstore I've ever in all my years seen. *Ever.*
DANIEL: Oh, I quite agree with you.
FLORENCE: Even here — in your own field — in your own professional area, you're incompetent. And you dare —
DANIEL: Now wait — this is not my drugstore.
FLORENCE: Ah-h . . .
DANIEL: One afternoon and four nights a week I labor here.
FLORENCE: Does your employer know what goes on in his absence?
DANIEL: I cured that ungrateful of high blood pressure.
FLORENCE: You . . . did . . . what?
DANIEL: My boss. My ungrateful neurotic boss. Look at this store! No goods on the shelves, no change in the register — no prescription labels, a Roumanian typewriter —
FLORENCE: You cured him of high blood pressure? High blood pressure?
DANIEL: The hard time he gave me — his own health, mind you. Took me years to convince him. And do you think he's grateful?
FLORENCE: *[Looking at him as if he were mentally deranged.]* I'd . . . better make my call. . . .
DANIEL: Yes . . . *[FLORENCE starts to the phone, but suddenly halts, overcome by a dizzy spell. DANIEL makes a move toward her. She draws away from him, getting, in the process a sharp pain in her foot and being forced to grab hold of a chair.]*
FLORENCE: I'll. . . . *[She fumbles in her bag, and comes up with a bottle. She takes a tablet from it.]* You have some water . . . please. . . ?

DANIEL: Right away . . . You should sit down . . . *[Again she draws back from him. He hastens back of the counter and through the opening to the sink where he draws a glass of water. She watches him. He brings the water to her.]*

FLORENCE: Did you wash. . . ?

DANIEL: It's clean. Very clean.

FLORENCE: Would you be kind enough to wash it. . . ?

DANIEL: It's clean . . . All right . . . *[He hastens back to the sink, washes the glass vigorously with soap, rinses it, is about to fill it with water, but then holds it up for her to see. When she nods approval, he fills the glass and quickly brings it to her. She takes her pill and swallows it down with the water.]*

FLORENCE: Thank you . . . thank you . . .

DANIEL; If you'll sit down . . . lean back . . . You'll feel much better . . .

FLORENCE: I'm all right . . .

DANIEL: I've a rocking chair in the back. Lean back for ten, fifteen minutes, your blood pressure will calm down . . .

FLORENCE: How . . . do you know I . . . ?

DANIEL: *[Pointing to her open bag.]* Raudixin . . .

FLORENCE: Oh-h . . .

DANIEL: If you took one Diauril now, right away —

FLORENCE: Are you prescribing for me?

DANIEL: You've heard of Diauril?

FLORENCE: I've taken it.

DANIEL: As a potentiator, no doubt.

FLORENCE: Certainly.

DANIEL: That's where the doctors make an error. You see, it's not only a potentiator. Not only that. More important, even, Diauril taken after Raudixin acts as an accelerator. It makes it act much faster.

FLORENCE: How do you know? How do you know?
DANIEL: I've tried it. I've used it.
FLORENCE: When. . . ?
DANIEL: My own high blood pressure. I made the discovery.
FLORENCE: *[Condescendingly.]* You . . . cured . . . your own high blood pressure?
DANIEL: Yes. Cured it — For all practical purposes . . .
FLORENCE: With all the doctors in the world unable to do so — you found a cure . . . I congratulate you.
DANIEL: I've some Diauril here, you can —
FLORENCE: Thank you.
DANIEL: I want to help you.
FLORENCE: *[Haughtily.]* Good day, sir.
DANIEL: Why don't you let me take your reading — your blood pressure? I don't think it's advisable for you to go out —
FLORENCE: *[Moving off anxiously.]* Thank you . . .
DANIEL: You shouldn't be going out there so soon —
FLORENCE: I'll handle myself, thank you. Take care of yourself.
DANIEL: By golly! I haven't taken my own reading today! Come on, I'll take my reading and then I'll take yours.
FLORENCE: *[Strongly disturbed.]* You'll take . . . your own reading?
DANIEL: Forgot all about it. Well-l. I can take yours, too.
FLORENCE: You can't. . . .
DANIEL: Come along. Watch. *[From beneath the counter he brings up a metal container and a stethoscope.]*
FLORENCE: *[Apprehensively.]* You can't, I mean you can't . . . take your own. . . .
DANIEL: Oh, I can't, can't I? Whoever told you that?

FLORENCE; *[Kindly — as to a feeble-minded person.]* Only a doctor can take your blood pressure.

DANIEL: Hooh, hah! Only a doctor! — Anybody can take his own blood pressure. I've taught hundreds of people right here how to do it without a doctor. I can teach you. Come . . . *[He lifts the sphygnomotonometer from its container.]* Watch. Watch how easy it is. Simple, nothing . . .

FLORENCE: You've got to have a doctor . . .

DANIEL: Any person half intelligent can do it. Observe . . . *[He sheds his coat, then rolls up the shirt sleeve of his left arm.]*

FLORENCE: *[With mounting apprehension.]* Don't you ever go to a doctor?

DANIEL: Regularly. *[Wrapping the cuff around the section of his arm just above the elbow.]* The cuff, when you wrap it — you have to be sure it's tight . . . tight . . .

FLORENCE: If you go to a physician, regularly . . . why do you. . . ?

DANIEL: Self-research. This is self-research. You must always do self-research. Now — we have to put this stethoscope under here . . . *[He inserts the flat disc of the stethoscope under the cuff just above the big vein opposite the elbow.]* Pump it up . . . *[He squeeze-pumps the rubber bulb.]* . . . See . . . Look . . . it's pulsing — the mercury. See where the mercury is pulsing? That's the systolic. I hear it beat–ing in the stethoscope . . . Now we'll loosen this screw . . . let out the air slowly . . . slowly . . . slowly . . . Ahhh . . . here . . . see. Here it holds, rests. Can't here anything in the stethoscope. Now we've got the diastolic.

FLORENCE: What did you get?

DANIEL: One hundred forty-seven over eighty-two.

FLORENCE: How can you accept that as valid? As having

any validity at all? You can't possibly —
DANIEL: Perfectly valid. My reading —
FLORENCE: Has no meaning whatsoever. None.
DANIEL: Why I've been doing this for years. Every time I go to my doctor our readings agree. A few points one way or another — which is natural — but never more. *Doctor-guarded self-research.* That's the only way you can really cure anything: self-research. But your self-research must always be doctor-guarded — checked by the doctor.
FLORENCE: *[Confused.]* I thought you didn't believe in doctors.
DANIEL: You can't get along without doctors.
FLORENCE: Then why do you set yourself up above them — with all their years of training, experience, resources? Prescribing medicines here —
DANIEL: The big trouble is with these know-it-all doctors. And far too many of them are too conservative, too timid, too one-track-minded and egoistic to be sympathetically intelligent.
FLORENCE: I haven't found that so. I've been to hundreds of doctors.
DANIEL: Hundreds?
FLORENCE: Yes, hundreds of doctors. All over this country. From Ohio to Maine, from Florida to the coasts of California. New York to Minnesota. Canada. And Mexico too. And Europe also. Half the world almost. I know doctors, I think. From long experience. So don't you tell me about doctors.
DANIEL: *[Impressed.]* Well, you top me, by golly, you do! I can match you from Ohio to Maine, from Florida to the coasts of California. New York to Minnesota. Mexico, too. I can match you there, I think, doctor for doctor. I can

match you there, I'm pretty sure. But you're ahead by
Canada and ahead by Europe, I admit. How are they in
Canada and Europe?

FLORENCE: What do you mean, how are they?

DANIEL: Better or worse?

FLORENCE: Neither better nor worse.

DANIEL: If I may ask — why . . . have you consulted so
many?

FLORENCE: *[Pointing to the blood pressure machine.]* Mainly
— this . . .

DANIEL: Where are you from?

FLORENCE: Ohio. Dayton, Ohio.

DANIEL: And you're here in New York . . . because . . . *[He
points to the machine.]*

FLORENCE: Yes. I'll have to make another appointment
now.

DANIEL: What for? You've already been everywhere. I
can help you cure it. Without any charge. I never charge.

FLORENCE: *[Intensely.]* Someone — there really ought to
be someone to stop you. . .

DANIEL: You're opposed to people being helped, aren't
you?

FLORENCE: Helped by qualified, competent persons,
not by *quacks.*

DANIEL: Why do you weigh so much? Your blood pressure
doesn't have much of a chance with all that weight.

FLORENCE: It's incredible that anyone like you —

DANIEL: You don't want to cure your high blood pressure do you?

FLORENCE: You should be reported to the police.
Someone should.

DANIEL: You really don't want to cure your high blood

pressure.

FLORENCE: Are you insane?

DANIEL: You're a perfectionist. You're looking all over the world for a perfect cure. There aren't any at the moment.

FLORENCE: Wasting my time — I — *[She turns to leave.]*

DANIEL: *[His voice pursuing her.]* Cut down your weight; cut out meat; eat fish; cut down your calories; get plenty of sleep, lots of sleep — *[Taking out his notebook and tapping it.]* — lots of rest in a chair. And love your fellow man as yourself. *[She turns on him a moment.]* Your fellow man as yourself. *[Tapping the book harder.]* And if you have the courage to do some self-research instead of hanging on to the coat tails of doctors all your — *[A middle-aged policeman enters.]*

FLORENCE: *[With an enormous sigh of gratitude.] Ahhhh* —

POLICEMAN: Got a rock in my eye, Dan! Wow!

DANIEL: *[Immediately ignoring FLORENCE in his concern for his new patient.]* Right this way, Al.

POLICEMAN: Hit me like a rock! *[Daniel takes a flashlight from a drawer and a magnifying glass. He hands them both to the policeman.]* Hold this a moment. *[The POLICEMAN takes the items. FLORENCE stares at all this open-mouthed. DANIEL pulls a piece of cotton from a dispenser, wets it under the sink spigot, then returns to his patient.]*

POLICEMAN: *[Wincing with pain.]* Phew-w. . . .

DANIEL: *[Taking the flashlight.]* Let me see. Hold this up here. *[The POLICEMAN holds the magnifying glass to the place directed.]*

FLORENCE: You have no right . . . *[But DANIEL and his patient are too involved to hear her.]*

DANIEL: Look up there. *[He points to the ceiling.]*

FLORENCE: You have no *right*. *[DANIEL, who is directing the flashlight at the eye and looking through the magnifying glass, suddenly makes a deft flick with the cotton swab.]*
DANIEL: Ah, that's an ugly cutey. Take a look at this one!
POLICEMAN: *[After blinking his eye several times.]* Now-w . . . that's more like it . . . *[Taking a look at the offending cinder.]* I toldja it was a rock! Br-r-r-. . . .
DANIEL: That one was easy.
POLICEMAN: You got that touch, boy. You're the only one. How come the others — they're all such cripples.
FLORENCE: He has no right to do this. It's against the law. *[The POLICEMAN looks at her for the first time.]* Removing foreign bodies from eyes, he's not allowed. I'm surprised that you — an officer of the law — aiding and abetting him. I'm shocked.
POLICEMAN: *[Sizing her up carefully.]* Well . . . it felt like a knife, miss . . .
FLORENCE: There are hospitals for such emergencies — just such emergencies. I'm sure *you* know of a hospital in the neighborhood close by. . . .
POLICEMAN: Dan's so good at —
FLORENCE: That's hardly meant as an excuse, is it?
POLICEMAN: *[Winking to DANIEL.]* Dan's a doc, miss. Dan's written a book on medicine. In fact, Dan, if you've an extra copy handy — I promised my missus I'd get her your book.
DANIEL: Well, I got a couple — a customer ordered two. But . . . I'll bring him another tomorrow. You can have one, Al.
POLICEMAN: *[Half-heartedly reaching for his wallet.]* I'll pay you . . .
DANIEL: My gift for your wife. With my compliments. *[He

brings up a paper-backed book from beneath the counter.] I'll
even autograph it in the bargain. *[He signs his name on the
fly leaf.]*
POLICEMAN: Fingerprints and all, huh. That's legal and
official.
DANIEL: *[Smiling ironically.]* We're always legal and
official.
POLICEMAN: Here's a man gives out more money every
day. Sam Berger got himself a job, he tells me. Because of
that money you lent him to insert his ad in the *New York
Times.*
DANIEL: The son-of-a-gun — I had to hit him on the head.
I had to shame him to his senses. One of those solid
naturalists, you know. He still believes in that dead-letter
idea: you're not supposed to tell people you're looking
for a job. It's not good manners. You only go out looking
when — only when there's a job listed. I shamed that
Victorian bugger into putting a Situation Wanted ad in the
paper. In two days he had a job! Two days. *[He has wrapped
the book, and now hands it to the POLICEMAN.]*
POLICEMAN: Yeah. Goes to show yuh. Thanks, Dan.
And thanks for the eyejob — boy. *[Quite embarrassedly, he
walks past FLORENCE and exits. There is a pause.]*
FLORENCE: *[Censoriously.]* You wrote a book?
DANIEL; I hope so . . .
FLORENCE: On what? What about?
DANIEL: It's all included in the title. "The Way To Health
Through Self-Research."
FLORENCE: Who published it for you?
DANIEL: Hah. I sent it out to fourteen publishers, but —
FLORENCE: So you published it yourself.
DANIEL: I consider it important, so — Yes.

FLORENCE: *[Graciously, understandingly.]* Sometimes that's the only way.

DANIEL: It's selling, so it must be useful, must fill a demand. If you read the *New York Times* . . .

FLORENCE: I do, I recall — Yes, I've seen your ad. May I . . . ? *[He hands her a copy of the book. She leafs through it with a professional air.]*

FLORENCE: This is probably the worst printing job I've ever seen.

DANIEL: Why?

FLORENCE: Why? Everything. Just everything jumbled together, pushed together. Awful . . . This cover, the back . . . page margins . . . the glut of italics . . .

DANIEL: I had to cut the book down. I cut a lot of material out.

FLORENCE: *[Reading something that has caught her attention.]* This reference to high blood pressure . . . You believe this? *[She indicates a statement on a page.]*

DANIEL: *[Reading where she points.]* Yes . . . of course. . . Everything in my book —

FLORENCE: How do you know?

DANIEL: Experience . . . it says there . . .

FLORENCE: *[Evenly.]* But it's not true.

DANIEL: Oh, yes, yes . . .

FLORENCE: I say it's not true.

DANIEL: I'm not the only one . . . other people have cor- roborated — You see there, I've advised other people . . .

FLORENCE: Nonetheless, it's not true. . . .

DANIEL: Well, could be . . . maybe not for you . . . but . . .

FLORENCE: Your book is a fraud.

DANIEL: Oh, wait a minute. Now wait. If you'll read,

you'll see —

FLORENCE: I've read enough already.

DANIEL: Oh, no, no. I keep warning the reader — you haven't read it. I keep warning the reader — You must always do self-research, keep trying different remedies, because what works for this person doesn't necessarily work for you. In fact, even more than that — what works for you today may not work tomorrow. Your own body — which you know best — better than anyone else — for the simple reason, the incontrovertible reason, impossible to deny — because you, you alone, always have your body with you, near at hand. It's better known to you than anyone else. Day to day, moment to moment. No doctor could possibly know it as well as you do. No doctor has the time, no doctor has the interest. It's your body. Your most precious possession. If you're ill, you feel it. If you're in pain, it's your ache. If you're well, your life's enjoyable. The rewards of self-research, on your own body, in the interests of your own health — the rewards are endless. And so satisfying, it makes you laugh, sing. Puts perfume into life. Because it's your own body, *yours,* which you know better than anyone on this earth. *[He points to a page in the book.]* It's all here. I say it here. Right here. *[She reads the statement, then looks wonderingly at him.]*

FLORENCE: Yes . . .

DANIEL: Are you married?

FLORENCE: I was.

DANIEL: Divorced. . . ?

FLORENCE: Yes.

DANIEL: Did you love your husband?

FLORENCE: At first.

DANIEL: That might explain it. Which could explain why

your high blood pressure — You didn't love him. Which
could be why in your case, sex, with him — sex, didn't
lower the pressure.

FLORENCE: Are you in the habit of giving things away?

DANIEL: What do you mean?

FLORENCE: That book. The money you lent to the man
to put that ad in the paper? Your free medical advice . . .

DANIEL: Each person finds his goal in life.

FLORENCE: *[Taking another look at the book.]* You have an
LLB after your name.

DANIEL: I'm a lawyer. I mean I graduated in the law. I
didn't like it. I had an office, but after six months. . . .

FLORENCE: Went from law to pharmacy?

DANIEL: Vice versa.

FLORENCE: Then why did you study law?

DANIEL: Pharmacy was not my first choice.

FLORENCE: No?

DANIEL: I always wanted to teach English.

FLORENCE: Then why didn't you?

DANIEL: My father talked me out of it. All those poems
in there are my own. In my class I use poetry as a basic tool.

FLORENCE: *[Reading from the book.]*

"This minute if I smile at once,

The sun of hope begins to flow,

And once we put a smile in tow,

There is no end to this response."

DANIEL: One of my most fundamental beliefs. Time and
again I've seen it work — I've seen it work. It was a great
psychologist —

FLORENCE: I know . . . You were so easily talked out of it.

DANIEL: In those days.

FLORENCE: And presently?

DANIEL: I'm set now. I don't teach English, but a class in morals.
FLORENCE: Are you married?
DANIEL: No.
FLORENCE: Ever?
DANIEL: No . . .
FLORENCE: You prefer to keep a mistress . . .
DANIEL: Oh-h . . .
FLORENCE: You're not a homosexual?
DANIEL: Oh, no, no — I'd never —
FLORENCE: But neither wife, and, I take it, no mistress?
DANIEL: Well . . . Hah-h-h . . .
FLORENCE: *[After a pause.]* Are you a saint, or a fraud?
DANIEL: Some of both. Why not?
FLORENCE: That's not what you say in your book; and your behavior here. Are you a saint or a fraud?
DANIEL: I try to live by a moral law.
FLORENCE: Which excludes sex?
DANIEL: No, I didn't say that. I couldn't have written about the lowered blood pressure . . .
FLORENCE: *[After another slight pause.]* I shall be in New York a week. I am staying at the Plaza Hotel . . . Sometimes . . . I get lonely . . .
DANIEL: You must never let loneliness get you down. There are always cafeterias, restaurants, libraries, museums, where people . . .
FLORENCE: At night . . . late at night . . .
DANIEL: At any hour . . .
FLORENCE: You wouldn't care to show me your city. . . ?
DANIEL: This is a bad week for me. I've got to prepare a radio program on my book. And I'm working on a paper for a speech to a psychologists' group on the value of

morals in mental health . . .

FLORENCE: I might stay another week. My time is my own.

DANIEL: You're very lucky. Mine seldom is.

FLORENCE: You're afraid of women.

DANIEL: No . . .

FLORENCE: I think you are.

DANIEL: No . . . no — it's just . . .

FLORENCE: I'll be free tonight. I'll be in tonight.

DANIEL: If I wasn't tight for time I'd be glad to . . . *[She looks at him evenly. He becomes uncomfortable. Suddenly FLORENCE crosses to the front door — and locks it.]* What . . . ? *[She pulls down the curtain on the door.]* This isn't my store . . . I don't . . .

FLORENCE: *[Moving back towards him.]* I can buy this store very easily.

DANIEL: But . . .

FLORENCE: *[Softly.]* My name is Florence . . . Daniel . . .

DANIEL: I'm responsible for . . . I . . . *[She merely looks at him.]* My boss . . . my boss might just — He does that some times.

FLORENCE: Oh . . .

DANIEL: Snoops around. Checking up —

FLORENCE: He does . . . *[She quickly picks up a chair, carries it to the door, and slips the back of it under the knob.]* Well, now, Mr. Boss, this does it for you.

DANIEL: Florence . . .

FLORENCE: *[Returning.]* Do you stand back of what you wrote in that book?

DANIEL: Course — of course . . . *[She rolls up the sleeve of her left arm.]*

FLORENCE: All right. Suppose then you take my blood

pressure now.

DANIEL: Now?

FLORENCE: Mmmhmmm . . .

DANIEL: It wouldn't . . . you, you — you can't . . . *[She looks around, spies the light switch on the back wall, crosses to it, and snaps off the electric light. The store is much dimmer. They stare at one another through a long tense pause.]*

DANIEL: *[Strongly moved.]* Florence . . . *[FLORENCE looks toward the back room.]* I . . . I . . . *[FLORENCE moves toward the back room.]* I . . . I . . . This . . . *[She disappears into the back room. He is completely unnerved.]* Florence —

FLORENCE: *[Off.]* Bring your blood pressure machine back here. *[DANIEL is speechless.]* Daniel. . . ?

DANIEL: Florence . . . *[There is a pause.]*

FLORENCE: *[Off.]* Dan-niel . . . *[Another pause.]* Dann-iel-l. . . .

DANIEL: Florence . . . I . . .

FLORENCE: *[Off.]* Dann-nn-n-iel-l . . .

DANIEL: *[Desperately.]* I can't . . . I can't . . . I can't . . .

FLORENCE: *[Off.]* Just bring your blood pressure machine . . .

DANIEL: I told you I can't — I can't — I can't! *[After a pause, FLORENCE reappears at the entrance way. Several of the buttons at the top of her dress have been opened.]*

FLORENCE: Daniel . . .

DANIEL: It's impossible . . . it wouldn't work . . . it wouldn't work. . . .

FLORENCE: *[After another moment.]* Why. . . ?. . . Why . . .?

DANIEL: It wouldn't . . . I can't . . . I'm ill . . .

FLORENCE: Where ill?

DANIEL: I, I've had an operation . . . you wouldn't be able to stand . . . Not that you don't . . .

FLORENCE: Yes?

DANIEL: You couldn't stand it.

FLORENCE: *[Haltingly.]* How . . . do you know . . .

DANIEL: *[Banging the wall behind him.]* God . . . God . . .

FLORENCE: *[Tenderly, sympathetically.]* What is it, Daniel?

DANIEL: Please . . . it's better this way . . . each person . . .

FLORENCE: Daniel . . . Poor Daniel . . .

DANIEL: Don't say that.

FLORENCE: I merely —

DANIEL: I stopped saying, poor Daniel, when I was nineteen years old. That's years ago.

FLORENCE: Poor Daniel.

DANIEL: Not at all, not a bit. I have my moments of despair, but I can always bounce back. Life works its way out. *[He turns on the electric light.]* My blood pressure's high now.

FLORENCE: I'm sorry.

DANIEL: What for? *[He takes a pill from a box in his pocket. He fills a glass with water at the sink, puts the pill in his mouth and swallows it down with water. Then he takes another pill from a second box in his pocket.]* Diauril. What I preach, I always follow. *[He takes the second pill in the same manner as the first one.]* Wait ten minutes. I'll take my pressure for you. It'll be down. *[He brings out his notebook and makes an entry in it.]*

FLORENCE: What did you write there?

DANIEL: Raudixin, Diauril, date, time, circumstances . . . why do you shake your head?

FLORENCE: Your self-research . . .

DANIEL: The most important therapeutic for any human being — physically, mentally, spiritually. . . .

FLORENCE: I'm afraid your self-research is simply an

illusion.

DANIEL: If you read my book you'd see that's not true.

FLORENCE: You're a fraud, Daniel . . .

DANIEL: I've been called many things, but not that.

FLORENCE: I do, because in the important areas you are ignorant. You raise false hopes. You talk, you advise, you write, you even help. And yet, you're a quack, a fraud . . .

DANIEL: Is it because you always want to run the show? Is it because you love yourself too much? Is that your trouble?

FLORENCE: *[Reflectively.]* In some ways . . . you are a remarkable man.

DANIEL: I make no claim —

FLORENCE: A remarkable man, in some ways. But you know so little about yourself.

DANIEL: You're wrong, oh very wrong.

FLORENCE: You say I love myself too much. You?

DANIEL: I only meant —

FLORENCE: I know very well what you meant, Daniel. Full well. I've traveled quite extensively, and I believe it's taught me some things. I do think you are a remarkable man, in some ways. A saint, in part, despite your illusions. And yet, still, before this week is out, I shall forget you. Even your book, if I read it — in a few months I'd not believe in it — however here and there it might be valid, useful. So, I will not buy your book.

DANIEL: Please let me give you a copy.

FLORENCE: No, it would do no good. I have already begun not believing in you.

DANIEL: Florence, please take my book . . . *[He extends a copy of his book towards her.]*

FLORENCE: I have traveled too much, Daniel. You are

what is known as a desert saint. You are merely a mirage. You see, I know your trick, Daniel. I have it myself, you see. I saw what happened when the policeman came in here; what happened when you went to the phone each time. I didn't exist when the others entered. I know the tribe of desert saints, I have their trick. When I leave here, you shall already have faded away. We had our moment, Daniel. It was not meant to be more. But we had our moment.

DANIEL: A moment can be everything.

FLORENCE: *[With a wise smile.]* Yes . . . Good-bye.

DANIEL: Good-bye. *[The phone rings. DANIEL turns automatically toward the phone. FLORENCE's smile broadens; she heads for the door. As DANIEL moves toward the phone, he stops suddenly to look at the departing FLORENCE. He shakes his head oddly, yet automatically extends an arm toward the phone, then turns and takes it. FLORENCE, as she reaches the door, and removes the chair, has already forgotten DANIEL. As she exits he speaks into the phone.]*

DANIEL: *[Having already forgotten FLORENCE.]* Orbit . . . Who . . .? Oh, what's wrong . . .? A little tincture of Merthiolate will fix that right —

CURTAIN

Move and
Counter-Move

CHARACTERS

FRED NOSSELL
HELEN NOSSELL
ARTHUR NOSSELL
JAMES ABBOTT
TOM HOYT

Move and Counter-Move

The living room of a home in the suburbs not too far from New York City. It is tastefully furnished.

FRED NOSSELL enters from the back.

FRED: Helen, where's the. . .? Helen . . . Helen?

VOICE OFF: Yes?

FRED: Where's the rubber-handled pliers I had?

VOICE OFF: What . . .?

FRED: The rubber-handled pliers!

VOICE OFF: In the garage!

FRED: It's not in the garage!

VOICE OFF: Maybe it's in your car!

FRED: It's *not* in my car! Have you been using it?

HELEN: *[Entering.]* What for?

FRED: Where is it? I can't find it!

HELEN: It'll show up . . .

FRED: I looked all over. Weren't you and Arthur using it that weekend on the lawn mower? Yeah-h . . .

HELEN: He put it back.

FRED: It's not there. I wish you'd put things back where

you find them. You and Arthur. No organization. . . .

HELEN: It's in the garage. Did you look?

FRED: It's not in the garage!

HELEN: It'll show up.

FRED: It won't show up! Nothing shows *up*! *[A pause. The doorbell rings. HELEN takes it.]*

HELEN: *[At the door.]* Yes?

VOICE OFF: Mrs. Nossell?

HELEN: Yes.

VOICE OFF: Mr. Hoyt suggested I stop past to see you. I'm from the Encyclopedia Britannica. May I step in a moment?

HELEN: Well . . .

VOICE OFF: I want to make a recommendation about your Britannica set. You have a Britannica set, haven't you?

HELEN: Yes. Yes, we do.

VOICE OFF: May I suggest something I think you'd find interesting? Mr. Hoyt did. And so did Mr. Hummer on Overbrook Road.

HELEN: Well . . . if you want to step in a moment . . . but . . . *[A young man enters with a briefcase.]*

JAMES: I'll only be a minute. Mr. Nossell?

FRED: Hi . . .

JAMES: How do you do? Mr. Hoyt told me you had a set. He just ordered a new set from me. He thought you might be interested in a new idea we're advertising.

FRED: Mr. Hoyt ordered a new set?

JAMES: Yes. We're getting an unusual response with this new program the Encyclopedia Britannica is present-ing. It's something special, something new. Nearly everybody we've shown it to has taken advantage of it. May I see . . . ? Oh, there it is. *[He crosses to the book case and lifts out a volume.]*

FRED: *[To HELEN.]:* Bill Hoyt's getting intellectual in his old age.

JAMES: This is a fine set you have.

HELEN: Yes, it is. It serves our purposes very well.

FRED: We're all lined up, young man. I wouldn't waste any time here, if I were you. Go to work on the neighbors around.

JAMES: I'll do that too. This set's been well used. I can tell that.

FRED: It's been used.

JAMES: Mr. Nossell, I noticed your new car out there. Don't make better cars than Oldsmobile.

FRED: Agreed.

JAMES: I think a man who buys a new car every year makes a smart investment.

FRED: Oh . . .

JAMES: Every year, every two years. You're always getting the top of the curve, the maximum from your car.

FRED: Look — cars and encyclopedias — they serve diffcrent purposes. Now don't waste your time, young man. That's the only commodity you've got to sell. Thanks for stopping in. *[He has maneuvered him so that he can only move toward the door.]*

JAMES: *[Easily.]* Thanks for letting me drop in. Thank you, Mrs. Nossell. *[He turns toward the door, almost reaches it, then casually turns around.]* You have a son going to Princeton, I hear.

HELEN: Yes.

JAMES: Would you be kind enough to tell him I dropped past. Here's my card. In case he's interested.

HELEN: *[Taking his card.]* Thank you.

JAMES: Mr. Nossell, may I ask you a question?

FRED: *[Who has already dismissed him and is preoccupied.]* What is it?

JAMES: You know, I meet a lot of people in my work. After awhile you get so you can tell what people are interested in what you have to offer, and which people are not. I've a hunch you'd be interested in the new Britannica. I think you would.

FRED: *[Looking at him pointedly, with a lift of interest.]* Would I?

JAMES: It's people who know their own minds who appreciate a reference book of this distinction.

FRED: You were going to ask me a question.

JAMES: Yes, I was. Would you give me fifteen minutes of your time — when you have the time — any time you name — You press the button — to let me explain this offer we're making? I think you'd be interested.

FRED: Now look; listen; move. I mean, I told you not to waste your time here. I appreciate your trying to make a sale. I appreciate that. But you fire your ammunition and juice on people who can use it.

JAMES: That's what Mr. Hoyt said to me, but all I asked him to do was listen for fifteen minutes. I'll compromise. Give me ten minutes of your time; any time you've got ten minutes. You press the button. Is that fair enough?

FRED: Yes, it is fair enough.

JAMES: Thank you. Thank you very much.

FRED: What's your name?

JAMES: James Abbott.

FRED: James, I'd give you ten minutes if it would do you any good. I would give it to you. Really — I mean that. But we're satisfied with what we have. So, I'm not going to waste another half second of your time — which you could use making a sale. Thanks a lot for stopping in.

JAMES: *[Aware that it is all over.]* Fine. Thank you. Mr. Nossell. Mrs. Nossell. Is there anybody on the block you think might be interested in having me drop in?

HELEN: I don't know. You might drop over at the Valentines. They're directly across the block. Two seventy-four.

JAMES: *[Making a note on a card which he has taken from his pocket.]* Thank you very much. Is there anyone else — ? *[The bell rings. HELEN takes the door. MR. TOM HOYT enters.]*

JAMES: Hello . . . *[He is making his way out rather hastily.]*

FRED: I hear this young man nicked you, Tom — sold you a new Britannica.

TOM: Sold me a Britannica? Not me. *[JAMES is already outside.]*

FRED: You . . . ? Hey, there . . . C'mere! C'mere! *[JAMES returns. Very unnerved.]* So you sold Mr. Hoyt?

JAMES: Well, you see. . . .

FRED: Throwing 'em wild, boy, 'll get you nowhere. Using peoples' names fraudulently 'll get you nowhere, and it's bad. Bad, boy; and no excuse. It only ends in defeat. I hate a bad salesman. Now you get out of this neighborhood. And I don't want to catch you going across the street — or anyplace. Is that understood?

TOM: Have you been going around here telling people I

bought books from you?

JAMES: I . . .

FRED: For the past ten minutes, he's been telling us you did.

TOM: I've a good mind to have you taken in. This kind of blatant knavery — this downright fraud — What's your name? . . . I said what's your name?

JAMES: James Abbott.

TOM: *[Writing it down.]* James Abbott. You clear out of these parts immediately. Your superior will hear from me. Trot, boy, and trot fast.

JAMES: I'm sorry to have troubled you. I —

TOM: That way. Now get. And trot fast . . . *[He points to the door. JAMES exits. A slight pause.]*

HELEN: Well-l . . .

TOM: Treat people decently, kindly. He said he'd sold a set to Arnold Hummer.

HELEN: I know.

FRED: Some kid.

TOM: Wonder how many others he's been twisting with my name . . . Fred . . . Howard Stand called me. Have you got a minute?

FRED: *[Surprised.]* Of course. Sit down.

HELEN: You don't need me.

TOM: *[Taking an arm chair.]* You won't be in the way. In fact, uh-h . . .

FRED: Sit down, honey.

HELEN: If it's all right . . . ? *[Takes a seat.]*

TOM: Fred, Howard you know, is on the board of my company, since last Wednesday.

FRED: Well . . . well, well . . .

TOM: I had to call him this morning, over a little business.
. . . He told me he's expanding International Products.
He feels his bottle-neck — what he needs, is a more active
sales force.
FRED: Yeah, we've banged that one up and around.
TOM: The point is — the point is Arthur.
FRED: What do you mean . . . ?
TOM: Why I wanted you in on this, Helen. I don't know
how we got on Arthur. We — When he heard he was
graduating school this summer, he told me he had an idea.
[Snapping his fingers vigorously.] His great forte. You know
Howard. . . . *[Fred nods.]* He wants Arthur to come in with
you people.
HELEN: Arthur? . . . Where?
TOM: I don't know.
HELEN: But didn't you tell him?
TOM: Oh, certainly, certainly — of course. But you see,
he, uh . . . asked me if I wouldn't release Arthur to him.
He put it to me as a special favor — a very special favor.
Well, I pointed out it wasn't up to me — I'd have to talk to
you.
HELEN: It's out of the question, Tom. Arthur's been
looking forward — he had his heart set on this. The last
time he was here we had a long talk —
FRED: We can always hear what Howard has to say, honey.
There's no harm in hearing what's on his mind.
TOM: You know Howard Stand. Once his prow is set.
He didn't get where he is now — Frankly, we're lucky to
have him with us. He was angry about something.
Something was-s . . . He said he wanted Arthur. He want-
ed Arthur. So-o — it's up to you and Arthur now. What-

ever you decide I'll go right along.

HELEN: But, Tom . . . if Arthur, if Arthur would prefer going with you. . . .

TOM: Anything you decide. *[The phone rings. HELEN takes it.]*

HELEN: *[Turning from phone.]* Fred . . . it's Howard Stand's secretary. Howard. . . .

FRED: *[Rising quickly and hurrying to phone.]* Hello . . . Yes . . . Hello, Howard . . . Yes, so I heard . . . Yes, this summer. . . . Yes . . . But I don't know . . . Oh . . . well, I have to . . . Yes, of course . . . True . . . Well, well, yes . . . Yes, sure . . . Sure . . . Good-by . . . *[He puts down the phone gloomily, then returns to HELEN and TOM.]*

HELEN: What did he want?

FRED: What Tom's been talking about . . .

TOM: *[Rising.]* Well, you and Helen, and Howard and Arthur kick it around. Whatever you decide . . . Bye . . . *[TOM leaves. HELEN and FRED bid him good-by.]*

HELEN: What did he say? Howard Stand? You're so glum.

FRED: No . . . no . . .

HELEN: Fred . . . ?

FRED: Was all fixed . . . this won't do . . .

HELEN: Then that's that. You'll tell Howard.

FRED: Impossible . . . just impossible!

HELEN: Why didn't you tell him? Then and there?

FRED: Of all the times. Damn . . . Damn-n . . .

HELEN: What's he want . . . ?

FRED: I mean it's — Damn, damn . . . what the hell —

HELEN: You should have made it very clear to him. . . .

FRED: Whatever put that idea in his head? Wherever . . . ?

HELEN: . . . You should have told him . . . *[The door opens. ARTHUR NOSSELL enters.]*

HELEN: Arthur . . .?

FRED: Son . . .?

ARTHUR: Mother . . . Dad . . .

HELEN: Is . . . everything all right . . . ?

ARTHUR: *[Unable to look at his parents.]* Great . . . just great . . .

HELEN: *[Covering her strong anxiety.]* We all have our days . . .

ARTHUR: *[Suddenly, to his father.]* Dad, have you been spying on me?

FRED: What?

ARTHUR: *Spy*ing on me?

FRED: *[Very carefully.]* Why . . . would I . . . want to do that?

ARTHUR: A lot of things I don't know why you'd want to do.

FRED: Son . . .

ARTHUR: Can't you keep off — leave me alone. I won't have anybody interfering in my life. Nobody, nobody!

FRED: All your mother and me —

ARTHUR: Dad, once and forever and for all — Now you listen carefully to what I'm saying. Carefully . . . Listen carefully . . . Keep your hands off. Let me alone! For God's sake, let me *alone!* *[HELEN looks perturbedly at FRED.]*

FRED: I wish I knew what you were talking about, son. I mean, I don't. . . . If there's anybody knows how to listen, that's your Dad. You can't take that away from me. *[Pointing to the sofa.]* Take it easy . . . Have you had your lunch?

ARTHUR: Boy, oh boy!

HELEN: Skipper. . . .

ARTHUR: — You, me, anybody. Automatic! Automation personified. *[FRED sits down slowly, his head in his hands.]*

HELEN: It's close to lunch. Have you eaten?

ARTHUR: He put his spies on me! Did you know that!? *[FRED looks up at him questioningly.]* Bob told me — Bob Anderhill. Bob told me how you approached him to get me on the student council. Bob told me! *[HELEN looks at FRED. He lowers his eyes.]* You bought Bob. Whatever — how — I don't know. What do you think I felt like when he told me I was a filler, because you conned him into the idea to get me on the student council. No, you wouldn't know. All your life you've been ramming things down peoples' throats. Ram, ram, shove it down their throats! That's all you know. That's all you live by! You didn't succeed! No, no! I'm not meshable, I'm not maneuverable, I'm not flexible, I'm not fitable! I'm never going to be either! *Never!* And *never,* and *never!* All right! I'm clearing out! And stay out of my way! Take your spies off me! I'll quit school, I'll clear out before June if I find anymore of this goddamn jazz going on! I'll quit! I'll quit! I'll quit!

HELEN: Son . . . what . . . what are you talking about?

ARTHUR: Ask him! If you can get a straight answer out of him, ask him! *[FRED makes a motion to his wife, indicating he doesn't understand.]*

HELEN: Son . . . I don't think . . . *[She looks at FRED again. He repeats the same gesture.]* Your father hasn't the least inkling what you're —

ARTHUR: He's lying!

FRED: Now, son. . . .

ARTHUR: I *know,* mother!

HELEN: All right . . .

ARTHUR: I'll say it again. He's lying!

FRED: *[Suddenly jumping up.]* I'll be damned . . . Arthur's right. The boy's right!

ARTHUR: *[Momentarily rattled.]* I'm . . . leaving now . . . You heard what I said.

FRED: — What he meant — that's it — Howard Stand. What do you mean, spying, son? People been asking questions about you?

ARTHUR: The questions *you* wanted answered.

HELEN: What do you mean? — Why would Howard — ?

FRED: I don't know . . . I . . .

ARTHUR: The man says — the man says he don't know. And it's all done with scotch tape — all of it! Daddyboy innocent, the face that's transparent. The baby-face move — He don't know. Everybody's a customer! God!! . . . I was so sick . . . I couldn't walk . . . back to the dorm. . . .

HELEN: Son. . . .

ARTHUR: How do you swallow this, Mother? *[They stare at one another, for seconds. Then HELEN turns away.]* Ask him, mother! You know the questions he wanted answered. Ask him what he found out. Whether I'm meshable yet — maneuverable, you know, *you* know! Good-by . . .!

HELEN: Son — *[But as his mother makes a move toward him, ARTHUR suddenly shoots out his arm against her in a flash of hard resentful anger. And for a moment the revealed antagonism of ARTHUR for his mother charges the scene. Then, awkwardly, his arm falls, he rocks indecisively. There is another painful moment. Then, impulsively, ARTHUR races off. HELEN hurries after him to the door. FRED grabs her arms, but HELEN struggles free and goes out to the porch. FRED stands disconsolately. Shortly, HELEN returns. There is a long, tense pause.]*

FRED: *[Deeply despondent.]* The way things come out . . .

HELEN: *[Too preoccupied — incoherently.]* There was this . . . he said . . . and then you . . .

FRED: *[Lost in his own thoughts.]* Tom . . . that phone call . . . all together — He, he wants Arthur to work for me . . .

HELEN: *[Confused.]* Who . . .? Work for you?

FRED: — On my sales force . . .

HELEN: What? . . .

FRED: My sales force . . .

HELEN: Howard . . . ? Selling . . . ?

FRED: Sell-ling . . .

HELEN: Arthur . . . ?

FRED: Arthur.

HELEN: *Arthur?*

FRED: This new sales program. That's the pitch.

HELEN: But . . . but, but —

FRED: It's tied in with this new sales program. Howard Stand's latest brain storm. They're calling them the guerrilla fighters. The guerrilla fighters. I told you last night —

HELEN: Last night?

FRED: You don't listen. See! *[Slamming his fist into his left palm.]* I told you he's calling them the guerrilla fighters! . . . The trouble is, there's a hitch, a bottleneck. They can't get college-trained men — we can't attract the college boys. He's gonna shoot only with college men in these guerrilla battalions . . . There's where Arthur — Wants Arthur to set an example. My son; Princeton man; working for me; sets and example . . . He sent somebody over to Princeton to find out about Arthur. That's what he did. So they told him — he found out the boy was on the student council, natural go-getter. Bang-g — whiz-bang!

HELEN: Arthur . . . ?

FRED: Hah! The student council. Hah . . .

HELEN: Did you. . . ? Were you . . . responsible?

FRED: I never dreamed . . .

HELEN: So you did.

FRED: Hell, it was the best thing happened to him. He needed it.

HELEN: But . . . but didn't you consider he'd find out?

FRED: I didn't consider anything. When he came out of that mental hospital all I could see was action. There was a job to be done — a wall to jump. I had to get him prestige — no matter how. I knew that was more important for him than all this flim-flam those doctors — I didn't like it. I didn't like him. That's right, Helen, I didn't like him. I knew in my guts, prestige was what he needed. Prestige — that's what he needed. Yeah — and it worked. It worked. You remarked yourself. Didn't you tell me yourself when he was home last time? Didn't you? *[She nods.]* If this hadn't come up with Howard now . . . God . . .

HELEN: But wasn't there some other way, Fred . . . ?

FRED: He's my son. Look, Helen, I — That's all we've got. . . . My son . . . my son . . . I couldn't — Not as long as I could help it. He was my son. He had to learn . . .

HELEN: *[Taking his hand.]* You and Arthur . . . sometimes I think . . . oil and water . . . *[He pulls his hand away with evident irritation.]*

FRED: I don't care what he thinks of me. . . .

HELEN: I do. . . .

FRED: Doesn't bother me. I've been mixing oil and water all my life. If Howard Stand hadn't come along now, now . . .

HELEN: Howard Stand . . . that man . . . He dominates your life.

FRED: Today.

HELEN: I wonder . . .

FRED: Tomorrow is what I'm looking at.

HELEN: If you hang around him long enough, by tomorrow. . . .

FRED: You've got to be meshable. You've got to have maneuverability. In twenty years he'll realize. Maybe when it's too late he'll understand. Anywhere, anyplace — you've got to be flexible, fitable. If it wasn't for that, how would I, me — with my background — *[The doorbell rings. HELEN takes the door. JAMES ABBOTT enters.]*

JAMES: *[Determinedly.]* Mr. Nossell. . . .

FRED: *[Harshly.]* What are you doing here?

JAMES: Mr. Nossell, I had to come back. The police picked me up. Did you . . . ?

FRED: Police?

JAMES: That's right. My boss had me released. Did you . . . call the police?

FRED: No, I didn't . . . I said I didn't.

JAMES: Then that means Mr. Hoyt . . .

FRED: Well, it wasn't me.

JAMES: I didn't see how you could. I didn't see how a sales manager could call the police.

FRED: How did you know I was a sales manager?

JAMES: When you're selling you have to know what you

have to know. I'm curious about people. You made a
mark on me.

FRED: I . . . ? How . . . ?

JAMES: You have a way about you, smart, sharp. I could
tell immediately in the technique you used, ushering me
to the door.

FRED: You went. I noticed, though, you turned around.

JAMES: Move . . . counter-move.

FRED: I ushered you to the door again.

JAMES: I went.

FRED: And then turned back again.

JAMES: To ask you a question.

FRED: Move — counter-move.

JAMES: You know the game.

FRED: *[Studying him closely.]* How old are you?

JAMES: Twenty-three.

FRED: Have you graduated high school?

JAMES: Oh, yes.

FRED: Any college?

JAMES: Nearly two years.

FRED: How much?

JAMES: About two years . . .

FRED: Actually, exactly — how much?

JAMES: Well . . . I had a year . . .

FRED: And?

JAMES: Went back a couple months.

FRED: Where are you from?

JAMES: Erie, Pennsylvania.

FRED: Where do you live now?

JAMES: In the city.

FRED: Your parents living?

JAMES: My father.
FRED: You want to work for me?
JAMES: Selling hard plastics?
FRED: *[Strongly.]* How much do you make a year? Exactly. Roughly?
JAMES: About ten thousand.
FRED: Ten thousand . . .
JAMES: I'll break twelve thousand this year, and more.
FRED: You won't make that with me for the first year, you know that?
JAMES: Well . . .
FRED: But there's a future. Promotion. A solid position.
JAMES: Yeah, I. . . .
FRED: *[Pointedly.]* You'll have to live here.
JAMES: Here . . . ?
HELEN: *[Perturbed.]* Fred . . .
FRED: *[Emphasizing.]* With us. Here.
JAMES: Why . . . ?
FRED: I want to train you — all around. *[HELEN stares at him frightened.]*
JAMES: But . . . I mean . . . ?
FRED: You'll use the name of Arthur Nossell . . .
HELEN: No!
FRED: You'll use the name of Arthur Nossell while you're working for me.
JAMES: I don't —
FRED: I'll make it worth your while. In ten years you'll have your own place like this.
JAMES: Mrs. Nossell. . . .
HELEN: I won't have it, Fred. It's out of the question! No! No!

FRED: *[Ignoring his wife — concentrating on JAMES.]* Agreed? *[JAMES stares at FRED with some anxiety and indecision.]*

HELEN: Don't do this, Fred. Don't — don't do this.

FRED: *[His eyes never leaving JAMES.]* It's settled? *[JAMES stares hard at FRED. Then, after a moment, he extends his hand.]*

JAMES: All right . . . *[Suddenly, HELEN strides out of the room. There is a charged pause. Finally, FRED points to the sofa. JAMES sits down; looks around the room carefully. FRED, observing JAMES' interest, uses the interval to pull himself together. Then, taking a chair opposite JAMES, he holds the silence, purposely, a while longer.]*

FRED: *[Now the executive.]* James, I'd better explain — *[HELEN enters with a travelling bag.]*

HELEN: I'll have to take the car . . .

FRED: *[Rising; carefully.]* Helen . . .

HELEN: I'm taking the car until . . .

FRED: I've got to, Helen . . .

HELEN: There's a limit. You'd go this far? Disown your own son? How much of yourself is still — Your own son? Make a stranger off the street your son!

FRED: It's a temporary maneuver. Howard Stand —

HELEN: Maneuver, maneuver, maneuver! I won't mesh that far! There's a limit to flexibility. Don't you know there's a limit? A limit!?

FRED: I'm only doing this for Arthur.

HELEN: I won't buy it. It's only an excuse, a rationalization.

FRED: Arthur can't work for me. You know that. But I'm not letting the boy down — which is what you're doing, Helen.

HELEN: What it all boils down to, Fred, is just that you're afraid. You're dead afraid, afraid to have it bright out and honest with Howard Stand. And there it is.

FRED: *[Hard, smoldering.]* Don't ever say that to me again. Don't you ever —

HELEN: You're blind there. You won't face it!

FRED: *[Too quietly.]* Who was it pushed that boy? And forced that boy? And ran him hysterical to private tutors, for years — from the time he was ten? You never let up. You kept the pressure on him. You wouldn't listen to me.

HELEN: That child had a natural gift —

FRED: That child had a natural appetite! No more than any other kid! But you wouldn't listen —

HELEN: I saw his potentialities. You couldn't —

FRED: So where did it lead!? The bug house!

HELEN: There's nothing wrong with him.

FRED: Is that why he spent five months —

HELEN: — He had a nervous breakdown. That's all. No more. He worked too hard. And this girl — Anybody would break down under such —

FRED: That's on your side of the family. Not mine. I don't have this in my family!

HELEN: *[Struck hard.]* You-ou . . . *[They just stare at one another. JAMES has been squirming on his seat; and now he begins to eye the door.]*

FRED: *[Nodding to end it.]* That's why he pushed you off. You saw him just now. . . . *[FRED shoots out his arm in the same gesture ARTHUR had made against his mother before he left. HELEN closes her eyes spasmodically. But in a moment the door bell rings. JAMES jumps up. The bell rings again. HELEN is fighting off a rising panic. FRED looks at her, then takes the door.]*

FRED: *[Speaking to someone off.]* Hello, Billy! You're collecting today aren't you? *[He takes change from his pocket and pays someone on the porch.]*

VOICE OFF: Thank you, Mr. Nossell. *[He is handed a newspaper. He stands at the door with the newspaper, then slowly closes the door. Heavily, brokenly, HELEN picks up her bag, stands irresolutely a moment, then crosses out right. She is heard climbing the steps upstairs. FRED listens, relieved. There is another long pause. FRED, bent, sorrowing, stares out the window of the door. Suddenly, he turns and catches JAMES peering at him. He peers back at JAMES. The two stare at one another like two fighters sizing each other up, maneuvering for advantage. Finally, FRED makes a move.]*

FRED: For a month you'll live here, get the hang of things, polish up, feel at home, till June. Then you'll come down the office . . .

JAMES: I'll be paid . . .

FRED: You'll be paid. Just learning . . . to be . . . Arthur Nossell . . . you understand?

JAMES: I will?

FRED: Yes. . . .

JAMES: *[Cunningly.]* How much am I going to get. . . ?

FRED: *[Tough; sharp; pointed.]* If you're smart . . . you won't take advantage . . . what you saw here — what you heard . . . till you're strong enough . . . to get away with it . . . If, you're smart.

JAMES: *[Staring at him a moment, then dropping his gaze — submissively.]* I . . . only asked . . . because . . .

FRED: *[His point made, and his pupil for the time being tamed, he gets right down to business.]* What's your name?

JAMES: James — Arthur Nossell . . .

FRED: *What's* your name?

JAMES: Arthur Nossell.

FRED: Where do you live?

JAMES: Thirty-seven Overbrook Road.

FRED: What's my name?

JAMES: Mr — *[FRED looks at him sharply.]* Fred Nossell.

FRED: What's my name?

JAMES: Fred Nossell.

FRED: What's my name?

JAMES: Fred Nossell.

FRED: What's your mother's name?

JAMES: Uh-h — Helen Nossell . . .

FRED: You're a graduate of — *[JAMES looks at him puzzledly.]* Princeton University. You're a graduate of?

JAMES: Princeton University.

FRED: What's your name?

JAMES: Arthur Nossell.

FRED: Your father's name?

JAMES: Fred Nossell.

FRED: Your mother's?

JAMES: Helen Nossell.

FRED: Yours?

JAMES: Arthur Nossell.

FRED: Address?

JAMES: Thirty-seven Overbrook Road.

FRED: *[Showing him a family album.]* Relatives . . .

JAMES: Right.

FRED: *[Opening the album.]* Your university?

JAMES: Princeton.

FRED: *[Pointing to a photograph.]* Your maternal grandfather.

JAMES: *[Looking hard; fixing it.]* Maternal grandfather.

FRED: His grandson's name?

JAMES: *[Like a shot.]* Arthur.

FRED: *[Still pointing to same photograph.]* This?

JAMES: His grandson? *[FRED nods.]*

FRED: *[The same photograph.]* This?

JAMES: His daughter. *[FRED's look, asking for more.]* My mother. *[More.]* Your wife. *[More.]* Helen. *[More.]* Likes to read. *[More.]* Likes me to read. *[A brief look of communion passes between them.]* Plays tennis. Grandfather too.

FRED: You too.

JAMES: I'll start tomorrow. This afternoon. Got a racket? *[FRED nods.]* You play . . . Dad?

FRED: Used to . . . son.

JAMES: We'll go out this afternoon. You can teach me, Dad.

FRED: Okay, son.

JAMES: What else, Dad?

FRED: *[Pointing to another photo in the album.]* This is your —

CURTAIN

What Do You
Mean By That?

What Do You Mean By That?

The living room of a spacious suburban home which, being near a heavily wooded area, suggests an air of a summer place. It becomes clear as the play progresses that the proscenium frame is really a picture window.

At curtain, GEORGE and ALICE are caught staring through the picture window as if each were alone in the room. Both are wearing shorts and cotton summer shirts.

ALLEN enters from the patio on the right.

GEORGE: *[To ALLEN offhandedly.]* What's he talking about now?

ALLEN: Who?

GEORGE: Him.

ALLEN: Oh-h . . .

GEORGE: What's he on now?

ALLEN: His income tax.

GEORGE: Talking about his income tax. That means he robbed them out of plenty.

ALICE: George . . .

GEORGE: He said he was talking about his income tax. What else?

ALICE: Every time you talk about your income tax does that mean you cheated them out of money?

GEORGE: I never talk about my income tax. Well, do I?

ALICE: Everybody talks about their income tax. Of course you do.

GEORGE: When *he* talks about his income tax, he rooked them out of plenty.

ALICE: Now isn't that ridiculous.

GEORGE: All right, all right. Come back in ten years. But remember what I said.

ALICE: Oh-h. . . .

GEORGE: Remember that occasion. *[CHARLOTTE enters.]*

CHARLOTTE: Alice. . .?

ALICE: Yes?

GEORGE: What's he talking about now?

CHARLOTTE: What?

GEORGE: What's he talking about? Him?

CHARLOTTE: Oh . . . nothing . . . his new motor boat.

ALICE: What's that mean?

GEORGE: Too easy.

ALICE: So?

ALLEN: Yeah, George.

GEORGE: It only means he thinks Boston is God's gift to the universe.

ALICE and ALLEN: *[Together.]* What!?

CHARLOTTE: *[Puzzled]* Would anybody care to. . .?

ALICE: Oh, one of George's clairvoyant days. ESP you know.

CHARLOTTE: Ah-h . . .

ALLEN: How did you sail up to Boston and that bit — from his motor boat?

GEORGE: Why the man's whole life is an adventure in creating little Bostons wherever he goes. Don't you remember — No, you don't. Well, twelve years ago he bought a place down near Brisbane, South Carolina, and he and a couple of his cronies didn't sleep, literally, until they'd turned that marshy hamlet into a miniature Boston. Restaurants, movies, stores, and a plastic model of the Commons.

CHARLOTTE: That sounds like any town. . . .

GEORGE: You'd have to had seen it.

ALICE: I saw it, George. The photograph.

GEORGE: And? Since you saw it?

ALICE: Well, now . . .

GEORGE: I specifically said miniature Boston. After all . . . he's the original despoiler of the American landscape.

[ALLEN has opened the door to the patio.] Allen. . .?

ALLEN: Yep. . .? [GEORGE motions that he close the door.]

GEORGE: What was he saying?

ALLEN: I didn't . . . no, he said something . . . the time when he was on the hill. . .

GEORGE: Hah!

ALLEN: Don't tell me you know what that means?

ALICE: George, will you stop it?

CHARLOTTE: You mean, you tell us — you know?

ALLEN: This I want to hear.

CHARLOTTE: Now stop looking like an owl. You know what he meant? "When I was on the hill. . ."

GEORGE: Elementary. Ask me something hard, chum.

ALLEN: Come, George, come. You're ducking.

ALICE: Serves you right. Let him have it, Allen. Go at him, Charlotte.

ALICE and CHARLOTTE and ALLEN: You tell us!

GEORGE: You all amaze me.

ALICE and CHARLOTTE and ALLEN: We know-w!

GEORGE: "When I was on the hill. . ."

ALICE and CHARLOTTE and ALLEN: "When I was on the hill. . ."

GEORGE: All it means — I tell the Senators *and* Congress-men what they better damn well do if they know what's good for 'em — if they want to *stay* . . . on the hill — that gravy hill . . . in Washington, D.C.

ALLEN: Eh-h-h-h. . .

CHARLOTTE: *[At the door and opening it.]* Hah, hah. . . *[A loud laugh, and then a voice from the patio.]*

VOICE OFF: —— What's good for 'em, if they want to stay on the hill, want to come back to Washington! *[CHARLOTTE bangs the door shut and stares at GEORGE. They all do. He takes it cool.]*

CHARLOTTE: George. . .?

ALLEN: Hey-y . . .

ALICE: Some people . . . are ver-ry lucky . . .

ALLEN: You've got to admit, Alice . . . George didn't know. . . .

GEORGE: I warned you it was pie.

ALLEN: How do you know all about this guy?

GEORGE: There are thing-gs . . . you know.

CHARLOTTE: How long have you known him?

ALICE: Hardly. Not really. Not at all. He just came over to ask about his car. He's staying with the Werkels next door. George doesn't know him all that. I've only met him twice.

ALLEN: What's that? What's this?

CHARLOTTE: For heaven's sake. It's amazing!

ALICE: *[To her visionary-attitudinizing husband.]* All right,

George. You can pose in this picture window.

GEORGE: Now you'll listen. Now you'll listen.

ALLEN: But how can you. . .? I mean, just by what he says?

CHARLOTTE: ESP?

GEORGE: Naturally, of course . . . ESP.

ALICE: You don't know a thing about ESP. I don't think he even knows ESP means extra sensory perception — that much.

CHARLOTTE: George . . .

GEORGE: Shall I tell you what Charlotte just meant when she said, "George?"

CHARLOTTE: Just "George". . .?

GEORGE: Oh, but you didn't mean — "Just George."

ALLEN: What did she mean?

ALICE: Yes, George, tell us. What did Charlotte mean when she said, "George?"

GEORGE: You really want to know?

CHARLOTTE: I'm dying to know.

GEORGE: Shall I tell you what you meant by that?

ALICE: *[Frightened suddenly.]* All right, George, this is enough. I think this has gone far enough . . . I've never seen him like this. I can't —

CHARLOTTE: No, I'd like to know.

ALICE: I really do think it's gone far enough. Really. Shall we go out to the patio? It's much cooler . . . *[She reaches the patio and opens the door for everybody to follow her. Suddenly a voice booms in.]*

VOICE OFF: —— Because when I leave Boston, I like to take Boston with me! I like Boston! I'm not your —— *[ALICE snaps the door shut! They all look at GEORGE now with amazement.]*

GEORGE: *[Laughing.]* There —- you see! You see! *[But he is somewhat startled himself at his own success.]*

ALICE: George. . .?

GEORGE: Darling. . .? Keeping our marriage salad fresh — hah. You keep the lady guessing.

ALICE: George. . .?

GEORGE: Darling. . .?

ALICE: Takes something out of you. It's a very funny feeling. You feel strange . . . very strange . . .

ALLEN: Well, I'll be damned, George. Hides his talents in the smokehouse, that boy.

CHARLOTTE: I know what you mean, Alice. The same feeling. Woo-oo, here.

GEORGE: Shake it out — it's just a game.

CHARLOTTE: But you said you could tell me what I meant when I said, "George."

ALICE: No, Charlotte. I've had it.

CHARLOTTE: It's very interesting.

ALICE: Do you mind, Charlotte?

ALLEN: What's the harm, Alice? She only said, "George." I'm curious. What could she have meant when she said, "George?" Just "George."

GEORGE: Shall I tell you what you meant by, "What's the harm, Alice? She only said "'George.'" I'm curious?"

ALLEN: Yeah-h . . .

ALICE: Please. Now I think this little guessing game has gone far enough.

CHARLOTTE: Oh, Alice, don't be a spoil-sport. It's just a game.

ALICE: It's not a game I like. George doesn't like that man. I know he doesn't like that man. Maybe it's easier when you don't like somebody. I don't know. What's gotten into everybody suddenly?

ALLEN: Nothing.

CHARLOTTE: *[Showing her empty palms.]* See . . .

ALICE: Well, I don't like it. I've seen this — All of you have. All people do these days — sit around analyzing everything, analyzing themselves and their friends interminably. It all begins innocently and for laughs. But I've seen it end in some nasty messes. Old friends breaking up. Because people have nothing better to do than sit around and undress and pull all their skeletons out of their closets and throw them on the floor. It's like a kind of cannibalism, a savagery.

CHARLOTTE: Oh, I don't know . . .

ALLEN: There's something to what you said, Alice, but this is different.

ALICE: I don't think so.

GEORGE: *[Sharply.]* Shall I tell you what you meant when you said —

ALICE: *No,* George. *No.* I'm not interested. I'm not.

CHARLOTTE: You know, Alice, I've watched these things. Sure it brings out some bloody things, and even bloody noses; but I've noticed, it's my experience, that people get to know each other better — what they really are; and they respect their weaknesses, the little clay feet in each other.

ALICE: That hasn't been my experience, Charlotte.

ALLEN: I don't think you can toss off an absolute statement about it, one way or another. It all depends.

ALICE: You'll excuse me then. And there are guests. . . .

[She makes her way to the patio again and opens the door. A voice off is heard.]

VOICE OFF: — I told that chap at the internal revenue, I told him it was all a mistake! There was no intent to defraud . . . *[All eyes are on GEORGE once more. But ALICE, after a moment's hesitation, continues on her way to the patio.]*

GEORGE: I better quit while I'm way ahead!

ALLEN: That's exactly what George said before.

CHARLOTTE: You mean he cheats — he cheats?

GEORGE: That guy? *Him?*

ALLEN: But how. . .?

GEORGE: Just listen. Every word he says. It's a cover for what he really means. Listen.

CHARLOTTE: This is uncanny. You're too smart, George, much too smart. It isn't fair.

ALLEN: Like Alice said . . . it hits you here.

GEORGE: Start listening. All you gotta do is listen.

CHARLOTTE: You promised to tell me what I mean by "George."

ALLEN: Yeah, yeah, yeah. You promised you'd tell what I meant by, "What's the harm, Alice? She only said, "'George.'" *[They both stare at him.]*

GEORGE: I was putting Alice on. Just pitching some good old woo.

CHARLOTTE: No, you weren't, George. This gal knows a woo when she sees one. And you're pitching me woo right now.

ALLEN: Com-me on, George.

GEORGE: *[Laughing.]* Shake it out — I was just having fun.

CHARLOTTE: Don't tell me, George.

ALLEN: You potted him right on the head, George, three strikes down the center right in a row.

CHARLOTTE: De-liver, George.

ALLEN: Cough it up, George.

GEORGE: Whatta you drinking, Allen? Charlotte?

CHARLOTTE: Now he's putting *us* on, isn't he?

ALLEN: You can't do that to us. *[They crowd him, one on each side.]*

GEORGE: *[Pointing out through the picture frame window.]* Did I tell you that tree over there —

CHARLOTTE: Get off that tree, George. You're being cagey, George. You are stall-ling, George.

GEORGE: I was lucky with that guy. Drinks?

CHARLOTTE: *[Grabbing his shoulder.]* I'm not going to let you off the hook, George. No, I'm not.

ALLEN: *[Awkwardly imitating his wife's action, and grabbing the other shoulder.]* No.

GEORGE: *[Flattered by CHARLOTTE'S display.]* What is this? O.K., O.K., send me a bill.

CHARLOTTE: I will. I mean I will. I will, George. *[They look at each other a moment oddly. The patio door opens. A short, fat man enters. They separate.]*

WALTER: George . . . Oh, there you are.

GEORGE: Another drink?

WALTER: I never refuse a straight offer like that. *[ALLEN and CHARLOTTE smile tightly. GEORGE starts to cross to the liquor tray.]* But, I've got the missus to meet. It'll have to be a rain check.

GEORGE: You bet . . .

CHARLOTTE: You're not leaving?

ALLEN: Not leaving us?

CHARLOTTE: You never did finish that income tax story.

ALLEN: Yes.

WALTER: Well-l, you know how the government is. Bunch of idiot beavers. The biggest bunch of idiots. You've got to waste your costly time, and time costs, straightening them out. High price lawyers you hire with nothing better to do. Claimed I owed them thirty-six thousand dollars. They weren't taking me.

ALLEN: What did you settle for?

CHARLOTTE: I hear those vultures always nick you for something.

WALTER: Settle for? I came out with them owing me money. I was too honest for those pygmy IBM sophomores. They owed me money.

CHARLOTTE: You hear that, George.

ALLEN: Well, now, George. They owed him money.

WALTER: I've got a standing philosophy. There's a light up here. When they call me in, they owe me money.

CHARLOTTE: You've been called in before?

WALTER: — And what you can't, just can't get through their plastic little heads is that money, money isn't money. You simply cannot make them see it that intangibles isn't money. Time, skill, insight, brains — they're intangibles, intangibles. And no brain-calloused government hack who works for me, tells me how to dispose of my money.

CHARLOTTE: Intangibles, yes.

ALLEN: Right you are.

WALTER: You just can't . . . make . . . them see it.

ALLEN: Talking about intangibles, George —

CHARLOTTE: Yes, George, Tell Walter. Now that's really in the area of intangibles.

GEORGE: *[Good-humoredly.]* When a man has a philosophy . . .

WALTER: A standing philosophy, George. And something I always make sure of. I don't go into anything, never do, ever, without there being a light up here. I work that out first.
CHARLOTTE: That's one for you, George.
ALLEN: There, George, there's one for you.
WALTER: George always leads with his lights on. Why he is where he is today.
ALLEN: So it's all done with lights, George?
CHARLOTTE: You turn it on, you turn it off — turn it on and off. So that's it, George?
WALTER: On the ocean you better not turn it off, you better make sure you're lights are working. They show you no mercy out there. Makes you realize the value of a clear philosophy.
GEORGE: Tell them, Walter.
CHARLOTTE: That's very interesting. You mean always, you always . . .?
WALTER: It's been the guiding notion in my life — and not to talk about myself — and I sometimes talk too much about myself. And I don't like that in myself — when I sometimes talk too much about myself I don't like it. But I mean I'd say, if somebody pinned me down as to the cornerstone of my creed: You work and make a light for yourself. Most people won't take the trouble — the work and the hard sweat to make a light, but you've got something, something that works when you're finished. You can even use it — proving how versatile it is, you can even use it when necessary to blind other people with, so you can knock them on their rear when they get too sharp and brassy. It's a two-edged sword. It's the greatest

philosophy I've ever found — and I've listened to a lot of 'em. In my business, the people I meet, there's always somebody shooting off his philosophy. I always measure them against my own, because I believe in that — you take all comers. Mine always won out. That's why they can't ever touch me at the income tax. I blind 'em in the eyes.

ALLEN: George said that. Everything you said! *[CHARLOTTE and GEORGE gape at ALLEN in surprise. CHARLOTTE kicks him.]* Well, didn't he? I mean George . . . *[He stops, his words hanging.]*

CHARLOTTE: *[Too airily.]* George knows everything. You missed a terrific game, Walter. Tell him, George.

WALTER: Well, George. What's this? What? What's all this game about my income tax?

GEORGE: *[Too smoothly.]* Oh, they're just talking about a game. These guys don't know it's something business people do off the top of the head, routine, all the time. In business you've to go with your sixth sense, you've got to be using extra sensory perception all the time. Makes all the difference between hitting it and sending back weather reports.

WALTER: Ah-h-h! Don't tell me about weather reports. There was a production man working for me once, and for seven straight days instead of progress reports all he kept sending me were sheets of medical statements on injuries, sicknesses, deaths, deaths, deaths. Don't tell me! What did George say, Allen, about my income tax?

ALLEN: *[Lost.]* Oh, oh —

CHARLOTTE: George wasn't talking about your income tax, Walter. *[ALLEN swallows. WALTER peers at him.]* He guessed everything you said, Walter. Everything. I've never, never, never seen anything like it. Tell him, George. Tell Walter. Tell him about the motor boat.

WALTER: What do you mean, guessed everything I said?

CHARLOTTE: Before you said it. Always before you said it.

WALTER: Before. . .? How did he know?

CHARLOTTE: I don't. We don't. And he's too crafty to explain. Hides his lights. You know about Boston — and how you like Boston?

WALTER: I like Boston. I don't care who knows it. I'm in love with Boston.

ALLEN: He knew you were going to say that, Walter. I mean George here knew it as soon as you mentioned your motor boat.

WALTER: *[Precise, sharp.]* He wasn't out there. You weren't —

CHARLOTTE: Exactly, Walter, precisely. What's so fascinating. I came in — I told him.

WALTER: About my liking Boston?

ALLEN: Nothing. Not a word. Just that you were talking about your motor boat.

CHARLOTTE: George, put it out . . . Tell your guest.

GEORGE: I was lucky, lucky. Anybody can do it. All you've got to do is lead with your lights on. Walter told you. You don't have to spell it out for Walter.

CHARLOTTE: But it was so perfect, George. I think Walter'd get a bang. Tell him, George.

ALLEN: Come on, George boy. This boy's a wizard.

CHARLOTTE: That's all he is. Leave it to George to surprise you with hidden talents.

WALTER: All of life's a game, ehh, George?

ALLEN: That was a pretty good game. A damn good game.

CHARLOTTE: As neat a damn game as ever I've seen. I mean when I came in he asked me what you were talking about, Walter.

WALTER: Ah-h . . .

CHARLOTTE: And all I said, all I said to George, I said you were talking about your motor boat. And George said, you know what George said? Look, you're not going to believe this, Walter. I warn you. I know you're not. I can tell you're not going to believe it. But Alice was here, Allen and myself. We were all here when he said it. When I told him you were talking about your motor boat, you know what George said? "Well, that means that he thinks Boston is God's gift to humanity." It struck me so funny at first. Wouldn't you?

ALLEN: ". . . to the universe. God's gift to the universe."

CHARLOTTE: Correct — right. That's what he said. *[A current of tension holds them in pause.]*

WALTER: Hah. Bob — Bob must have told him. Bob Werkel. Right, George?

CHARLOTTE: Next door? Over there?

WALTER: His neighbor, next door, Bob Werkel. Hah, hah. Good game. You had 'em all believing you were clairvoyant. Very good, George.

GEORGE: I've been telling them, trying to tell them.

ALLEN: We have been took, Charlotte.

CHARLOTTE: All that ESP was only his neighbor. . .?

ALLEN: We have been took. Now you see it, now you don't.

CHARLOTTE: George, there's a word for people like you. *[GEORGE smiles lightly. But there is an awkward pause.*

ALICE enters.]

ALICE: George, would you make Jean her favorite.

GEORGE: Coming up. Who else? Charlotte? Walter? Allen?

WALTER: Skip me.

ALICE: *[Pointing through the window.]* Without that chestnut everything has become so totally different. We had perfect privacy. And poor Cassy and poor Bob —

GEORGE: Was over a hundred years old, and boom! In ten seconds it cracked down, flat, dead. Gone in ten seconds flat!

WALTER: Was there anything else I said that George could tell what I meant? Looks like you had a rattling good game on me.

ALICE: What?

WALTER: I'm told George is a wizard — George can tell what a person means underneath what they say, as soon as they say it.

ALICE: Oh, George's little game.

CHARLOTTE: Only it's no game, Alice. Only your next door neighbor who punched all his cards. George was royally pulling our legs.

WALTER: Has Bob been telling you anything else about me, George?

ALICE: Bob? *[She looks at GEORGE and then WALTER.]* Bob never talks about you Walter.

WALTER: Well, you know how it is. I'm an old friend of Bob's.

ALICE: Bob has never said a word about you that wasn't to your credit.

WALTER: But you said he never talked about me.

ALICE: In that way, I meant. In that way.

WALTER: Being an old friend of Bob's, and friendship is something to me of sterling value — (if you knew me you'd know that) — I value friendship as Bernard Shaw said; so maybe as old friends yourselves you ought to know I saved his neck a couple of years ago. His business — you might even say, everything he has, the whole package. His home, his wife, his summer palace here, you might say he owes all of it to me. I bailed him out, I did that, I lent him money, and I did that when his creditors were hollering — that boy is bankrupt. The pack, the whole pack, George. Now there it is, all still through this picture window here. Beautiful isn't it? You can appreciate it now. Altogether one beautiful sight.

ALICE: Bob has never said a word about you, Walter. Never a word.

WALTER: Seeing it from here it's as if, you have that omnipotent feeling you could pick it up. Have you felt that, George, with the chestnut tree down, gone? *[GEORGE is silent, strained. WALTER stares at him sharply.]* He owes me a whole lot to be quite frank, I'd say.

ALICE: Now, George, you know Bob —

GEORGE: *[Brusquely.]* You told the man. You heard Alice.

WALTER: I did. I did.

ALICE: George . . .

GEORGE: *[Incisive, coldly.]* What is it, Alice?

ALICE: You're . . . giving the impression. . . .

GEORGE: Is that what you think, Walter?

WALTER: Well-l . . .

GEORGE: You're wrong, if you do.

WALTER: That's A-A-A enough for me. Because there's

no occasion. I mean, you understand that, George?

ALICE: Be sure of one thing, Walter. Bob never talks. I keep repeating — We're old friends of Bob and Cassy. We're the best friends they have. Bob couldn't talk about a friend behind his back. It's not in him. Not Bob. *[After a tense pause — ALICE looks worriedly at GEORGE. ALLEN and CHARLOTTE peer uneasily at ALICE — then at GEORGE, then, as an afterthought, at WALTER.]*

WALTER: I'll be off. Thanks . . . for everything. *[WALTER starts off, then stops in front of the picture window.]*

ALICE: Good-by . . .

WALTER: *[Pointing to picture window.]* Oh, yes. I forgot. Looking out there — I was going to tell you this story — forgot the story. Ah-h, yes, yes, yes. Getting it from here . . . Alice, Alice, yesterday morning I saw you, Alice, looking through this window, in the morning. And then, in the evening, yesterday that evening, there was George, George, standing here, looking through this window. And I —

ALICE: There was always the tree before. We haven't —

WALTER: —And seeing George, here, George at evening, suddenly brought it back. The memory — the whole-le story — in a flash. Well you know how a flash of memory — The way you all felt when Charlotte, when Charlotte said I was talking about my motor boat. That's the way it was — seeing you and George in this window. It's the story of an old friend of mine who built himself an imposing, magnificent home square on the top of a hill with a view that was something splendid to see. And then right across the valley — oh, wasn't too much of a valley, because it was all, all right in the same town, he bought another place —

much more modest, but very nice and decent, middle class — a home for his mistress. For his mistress — right under his wife's and his family's nose. Now he often, he very often worked upstairs in a special room, even though his wife was a millionaire; and his mistress, she always knew when he was coming to see her if he sat by the window in the evening at seven reading his newspaper — at the window reading his newspaper at seven. Fifteen years this went on, lasted fifteen solid years, this perfect — perfect, clever, silent communication between their two windows. I mean you see how I was reminded of my friend, seeing you at the window, George, in the evening. And . . . since his name was George, you can appreciate the way it struck me there, seeing George here . . .

GEORGE: And especially since I'm the one, I'm the boy, had this window put here. Right, Alice.

WALTER: Cassy and Bob told me that, yes-s. . . . But seeing you both here — I thought you'd enjoy that little story. Thanks for everything. *[WALTER departs. There is a pause.]*

ALLEN: Well-l — so. That's how come. You knew all about that shrewdy buzzard, you stinker you. You're a skunk, George.

CHARLOTTE: Well-well, well-well. Took us in like a bunch of

ALICE: Bob has never told you anything. Nothing.

ALLEN: Al-lice!

CHARLOTTE: Hear — hear-r!

ALICE: Didn't he say he knew what you meant by, "George?" Did you talk to him?

CHARLOTTE: Yes-s-s. . .?

ALICE: Did he talk to you, Allen?

ALLEN: No-o . . .

ALICE: I don't know what got into him. Oh, not like this. Ever since he's become executive vice president — I don't know . . . something. . . .

GEORGE: *[Pointedly.]* What makes you so sure Bob doesn't talk?

ALICE: *[Perturbed, puzzled.]* What?

GEORGE: So sure?

ALICE: Are you all right?

GEORGE: So perfectly, per-fectly, sure?

ALICE: H'm . . . well. It's all beyond me.

CHARLOTTE: Of course, he did.

GEORGE: Maybe he didn't, Charlotte.

ALICE: No question at all, he didn't.

CHARLOTTE: Did he, or didn't he? Stand up, George. Stand up.

ALLEN: *[Heatedly, arrogantly.]* Yeah, George, stand up, boy. *[GEORGE looks at ALLEN. ALLEN faces him coldly.]*

ALICE: These games. I tried to tell you it was time to stop. It's bad enough when people hurt themselves with their eyes wide open, but when some poor innocent — entirely innocent, has his reputation hurt, that is going too far. Much too far.

GEORGE: I told him Bob told me nothing.

CHARLOTTE: George-ge . . .

ALLEN: But the way you told it. There should have been no doubt in that man's mind.

GEORGE: No fault of mine is it, am I to blame if that shark's mind is devious. Why do you think he told that story? Just like that!

ALICE: Allen . . . Charlotte — what did you think?

GEORGE: Yes. Now it's your turn to tell George what he really meant. You see how easy it is. You tell George what he meant. Well, Allen?

ALLEN: Look, George. . . .

GEORGE: Charlotte?

CHARLOTTE: You certainly told him. But now —

ALICE: Well, I don't think he did.

GEORGE: *[Acidly.]* You wouldn't.

ALICE: What do you mean by that?

GEORGE: I usually say what I mean.

ALICE: Full of games today, isn't he?

ALLEN: You sure are, George. You sure are, boy. Walter's too much for you.

GEORGE: What do you mean by that?

ALICE: Here we *go* again!

CHARLOTTE: If you hadn't put your big foot in it. Leave it to Allen dearie to put his big-g foot in it.

ALLEN: George said he cheated on his income tax, didn't he? Didn't George say that! Didn't he!?

CHARLOTTE: Why, Allen, everybody all the time, says everything, Allen, everyone does constantly, Allen, everyone I know is always saying something, Allen, all kinds of things — everything and anything about their income tax. Don't you?

ALLEN: Look . . . here . . . Charlotte, now look . . . Don't try that. Don't put me in the wrong. *[There is a spark of tension.]*

CHARLOTTE: When Allen my pet gets sulky it's time to take him for a drive. Anyhow, it was lotsa fun, Alice. *[She turns to ALLEN.]* We've got to go, Allen love.

ALLEN: Alice . . . it was . . .

CHARLOTTE: A lot of fun.

ALICE: Well . . . Thanks for dropping over . . . *[ALLEN and CHARLOTTE wave, and go off. There is another tense pause which ALICE tries to cover by too carefully picking up glasses and things.]*

GEORGE: *[Finally.]* Nice show you put on . . .

ALICE: *I* put on.

GEORGE: Oh, very nice.

ALICE: Bob has never said a thing to you about Walter.

GEORGE: Has he to you?

ALICE: Why me?

GEORGE: Shall I tell you what you mean by that?

ALICE: I wish you would.

GEORGE: Really. . .?

ALICE: So?

GEORGE: The obvious, lady, is for idiots.

ALICE: Meaning? . . . Go on. *[A slight pause.]*

GEORGE: *[Suddenly.]* You hear that?

ALICE: What?

GEORGE: Listen . . . listen . . . *[A slight pause.]*

ALICE: That's Walter . . .

GEORGE: Bob and Walter. Walter, Walter and Bob.

ALICE: Oh, that's terrible. Terrible. *[Looking out the window.]* They're going to fight!

GEORGE: Good. Boof-f! Hah-h! Hah-hah!

ALICE: My God . . .

GEORGE: Only they won't, they won't . . . Walter knows damn well, he knows damned well, Bob'd kill him. *[He turns away from the window. In a moment the roar of a motor is heard.]* Told you. Hah! The strategic retreat. There. . . .

ALICE: You're a rat if I ever saw one.

GEORGE: You mean town rat or-r country rat?

ALICE: Miserable rat!

GEORGE: What does that make you, Alice?

ALICE: Now look here —

GEORGE: You can dish it out, can't you. Well, I don't like Bob, uh — how shall I put it? — being so neighborly and so palsy close to you. He won't be here next year.

ALICE: What does that mean?

GEORGE: You tell me, mate, what does it mean?

ALICE: You don't love me. What difference does it make to you?

GEORGE: I don't like Bob. *[They both stare pointedly at one another.]* The least my wife might do is be original.

ALICE: What game are you playing now, George?

GEORGE: Whatever game you like, Alice.

ALICE: *I don't play games. Never.* Since they made you vice president you have become impossible. It's gotten to the point now —

GEORGE: Don't change the subject.

ALICE: This is the subject. You carry yourself —

GEORGE: I was talking about you and Bob.

ALICE: Maybe I might talk about you and Cassy.

GEORGE: You can talk about anything you want to, but what's been pointed at you, as you always do. Always as always. *[He starts for the patio.]*

ALICE: Why are you running away as soon as I mention Cassy?

GEORGE: *[Pointing to the patio door.]* Jean is out there.

ALICE: Jean went down to the garden. *[He continues to the patio anyhow.]* Where are you going?

GEORGE: Where?

ALICE: And why?

GEORGE: O.K., Alice. I told you about Bob, and that is that. I don't want one of your endless rigmaroles — interminable, justifying yourself! God! Not that game!

ALICE: Any games I know I've learned from you.

GEORGE: Oh-h-h . . .

ALICE: Your games. They're your games.

GEORGE: You infect very easily . . . don't you?

ALICE: Maybe I do.

GEORGE: Maybe!? Hah! All the time. You . . . just . . . infect. "I don't like this game. These games." It's all the time. *Everything!*

ALICE: What do you mean by that?

GEORGE: God-d . . .

ALICE: I asked you what —

GEORGE: *Anything — Any*body!

ALICE: Was there . . . ever anything between you and —

GEORGE: Anything and anybody!

ALICE: I am asking you if there was ever —

GEORGE: A bastard. A bastard!

ALICE: *[Narrowly.]* What . . . bastard?

GEORGE: *That* bastard.

ALICE: Is there? Is there something —

GEORGE: I *told* you he was a bastard. I can spot them like that! Right off. Didn't I spot him — didn't I tell you right off that shark was a bastard? I told you what he was, didn't I? That story he told Bob. I'll bet you, I'll bet you anything you wanna bet there's not one straight word in it. Every word he says. He probably once, he probably lent Bob ten bucks once. Coming out that way to us, to strangers, to strangers, about Bob, his sterling friend, Bob, and all that horseshitty crap about friendship, and Bernard Shaw that he picked up from a book of quotations. He's the kind of barracuda that even barracudas hate.

ALICE: Was there, George?

GEORGE: What . . .?

ALICE: Between you and Cassy. . .?

GEORGE: Me . . . and Cassy.

ALICE: Was there?

GEORGE: Was there what?

ALICE: I'm asking you.

GEORGE: Oh-h, that's why. I see! I get it now! Oh-h-h! Ah-h-h-h! That's why I had that window put there, didn't I, Alice? Knocked that wall out. Ahah!

ALICE: Why don't you answer my question?

GEORGE: All-l that time. Right, Alice? So *now* we know. *[She studies him through a pause. He points to the left.]* You wanted it there, didn't you? But every time, every time I asked you why, why you preferred it there, to give me a reason — *one* reason — you just wanted it there. But why did I want the window installed on this side? Why? Or don't you remember?

ALICE: You're just avoiding answering my question.

GEORGE: I'm asking you a plain, simple question. Now tell me why.

ALICE: You won't answer it, will you?

GEORGE: Answer . . . what . . . Alice?

ALICE: All right . . .

GEORGE: All right, what. . .?

ALICE: H'mmm . . . yes . . . I am begin-ning to understand.

GEORGE: Oh, boy he picked you. I'll say that for him. Boy, you . . . take all-l the marbles. Blind 'em right in the eye — that's Walter Sykes — right-t in the eye. The quick innuendo, the shot in the dark — any shot in the dark. And you . . . you fell hook, line and sinker — swallow it exactly as he calculated. Yes mam, Dolly, you get *all-l* the marbles.

ALICE: There is . . . something going on between you and Cassy, isn't there?

GEORGE: Walter Sykes said so, didn't he?

ALICE: He didn't have to.

GEORGE: Ah-hah!

ALICE: And nobody blinds my eyes.

GEORGE: No-o-o . . .

ALICE: Nobody.

GEORGE: *No-o-o . . .*

ALICE: I've had this feeling for months . . . I was almost certain. Something went off between you and Cassy . . . didn't it?

GEORGE: Roll on, Alice.

ALICE: And that's why *you* — *you* don't want them here. Because of Cassy. That's why isn't it?

GEORGE: [*Walking woundedly up and back across the room.*] Keep shooting, Alice. Right off the top, baby.

ALICE: You're more devious than Walter — than Walter Sykes aren't you?

GEORGE: Heads up, Alice. Hell, you can top that.

ALICE: When it comes to the marbles, they're holding them all for you. Because the way you play, the games you play, you're going to get the whole bag. Right to the top. And then you'll be there all alone.

GEORGE: Good. Very good.

ALICE: What do you mean by that?

GEORGE: It amazes me. I'm stunned. Blind. I mean what do you say? Living with a woman fourteen years, and you don't know a thing — don't know her — you realize suddenly, you know nothing. Noth-ing. I cut a window here instead of where she wanted it, because I love a chestnut tree — which only happened to be one of the most superb, one of the finest chestnut trees I've ever seen. Which my wife knows, which I was certain she knew absolutely — if you can be certain of anything anymore. And then one night six years later, six years afterwards, after the window was cut, a storm in the night knocks the tree down. And suddenly, lo and behold, we can see our neighbors, and our neighbors can see us. And that's why I had the window cut here. Ah-h, ah-h — one of George's games. All that time. That . . . is . . . why. So I could read my newspaper here at seven o'clock.

ALICE: You're quite a bastard, George. You're a bastard. *[They glare at one another from opposite sides of the room. Suddenly, ALICE sees something through the window.]* There she is. Your buddy, your buddy gourmet, your witty, effervescent girl friend. Don't you want to take a look at her? Don't you, George? *[ALICE is standing in front of the window and pointing straight out challengingly.]*

GEORGE: Stop that.

ALICE: She's still there, George. She's waving. To you. Of course.

GEORGE: What the hell's the matter with you? Will you stop being an idiot?

ALICE: Hurry, George. Hurry. Oh, come, why this sudden rash of bashfulness? I know, I know it's not exactly seven, but when did time ever trip you?

GEORGE: This is the stupidest, most stupid — We've got to go over there, you know.

ALICE: [*Suddenly remembering.*] I am not going.

GEORGE: We're invited for dinner. I wasn't the one —

ALICE: What do you mean by that?

GEORGE: It wasn't me . . .

ALICE: Just what does that mean?

GEORGE: Look here, Alice . . .

ALICE: I'm asking you *what* you mean by that? What do you mean by that? [*GEORGE stares at her with a kind of helpless air, like one who has started something that is getting out of his control.*]

GEORGE: I said —

ALICE: I'm waiting for you to tell me what you mean by that? And where is the screen you were going to put there? I notice you never put it there. I notice that. You brought it in, but there it sits. Over there. I notice that.

GEORGE: I told you I wanted to clean it off —

ALICE: That was four days ago. You only say you're going to do things. You talk a good game. You do that, don't you, George? You and Walter. You talk a ver-ry smooth game. [*GEORGE crosses to the screen, at the back of the room left, picks it up and carries it across to the window. He doggedly screens off the picture window. But the audience can easily see GEORGE and ALICE through the openings of the screen's segments.*]

ALICE: Anything that's convenient for you; George, you'll do anything that's convenient, won't you? *Any*-thing.

GEORGE: What is it you want, Alice?

ALICE: What do you mean by that?

GEORGE: Look —

ALICE: I am looking. I ask you what you mean by that?
It's your game isn't it? What do you mean by that?
[GEORGE sinks into the sofa, sunk in gloom.] Don't you know,
George, what you mean by what you say? Don't you know,
George, what you mean by what you do? *[She stands over him
angrily.]*
GEORGE: I notice . . .
ALICE: What? What do you notice? What do you mean
by that? What do you mean by "I notice"? What is it that
you notice? Have you ever, ever noticed that for years,
years, years, you've been telling me how nimble and quick
and bright and charming, charming, *charm*-ing smart you
are. That you, you have a sixth sense about people, can
spot them right off! And you, you know how to pitch the
old woo to always get what you want. And that you, oh yes,
you, know how to turn it off and turn it on. And it was you,
you, *you* who cut out this wall here and put this window
here. You've had quite a long, long run with your *me, me,*
stories haven't you? The longest run in history — fourteen
years. No, longer, longer — even before our marriage —
longer. I don't want to mar your record. How bor-ring.
God, how boring, boring, boring, boring! Day after day-y,
the same deadly stories about George's "Look-at-me"
tactics. Oh, how bor-r-ring. Boring, bor-r-r-r-r-r-ring!!!
[GEORGE is sitting on the sofa, baleful and taut.]
GEORGE: *[Rising on a slight pause.]* You're just like Walter
aren't you? Hnh.
ALICE: *[Blazing.]* What . . . do you mean by that?
GEORGE: I mean by that, I mean you're full of lights —
lit up full blaze. You've got all the lights.
ALICE: You can't take it, can you?

GEORGE: *I* can't take it. Who's the one, who is it, who's the one gets these fancy-lovely all-day moods. These beautiful moods?

ALICE: You have to be able to feel something to have a mood. It takes sensitivity and intelligence and concern, con*cern* for something and somebody besides yourself. *[The phone rings. And having landed the last crack ALICE sails to the phone.]*

ALICE: *[On phone.]* Hello . . . *[Immediately gracious.]* Oh, hello, Bob . . . *[GEORGE is all ears at once.]* Well . . . Well . . . *[Becoming tense.]* I would rather we . . . I don't . . . I did not . . . I tell you I didn't say a . . . Do we have to discuss . . .? I, I, I . . . What do you mean by that? . . . No, I don't talk in my sleep . . . I told you I did not . . . I never talk in my sleep . . . What do you mean by that? . . . I have told you . . . I've nothing more to say now . . . I don't want to talk about it now . . . I cannot talk now . . . I can't . . . *[She listens a long moment, then slowly lowers the receiver to its cradle. ALICE is immensely distraught and crestfallen. There is a strong charged pause.]*

GEORGE: *[Finally, and acidly polite.]* I did my best. I tried, I tri-cd to tell you. *[ALICE is too intensely disturbed to talk. Suddenly GEORGE hears something. He listens, then crosses, moves the screen and looks out. ALICE, too, looks out the window, becoming acutely interested.]*

ALICE: What. . .? What is that?

GEORGE: Hnh.

ALICE: *[Looking at him curiously.]* What's . . . going on?

GEORGE: *[The wounded husband again.]* Here, I want out, I want out — Hah!

ALICE: *[Pointing out.]* A blue spruce. . .? . . . A blue . . .

spruce? *[He preens his hurt.]* Why, George? Why did you buy a blue spruce?

GEORGE: Yup . . .

ALICE: Because I like a blue spruce, George? You bought a blue spruce now, finally, for me, for me?

GEORGE: *[Giving up]* Oh, boy.

ALICE: Or could it be because . . . maybe because you feel guilty . . . George? Guilty?

GEORGE: *[Startled.]* How. . .?

ALICE: Guilty . . . guilty.

GEORGE: *[Trapped, caught, showing it.]* Hah. . . .

ALICE: *[Throwing it at him hard.]* Yes . . . yes . . . yes . . . *yes*-s-s

GEORGE: *[Fumbling awkwardly.]* You . . . you . . . think . . . .

ALICE: So-o, you see, you see, *I know* what you mean by *what you do.*

GEORGE: *[Suddenly becoming amused.]* Oh-h-h . . .

ALICE: And also, also, I *know* what you mean by *what* you say.

GEORGE: *[Dripping irony.]* Obviously — *ob*viously.

ALICE: So it was you and Cassy. It was. You and Cassy.

GEORGE: *[Strangely amused.]* And, uh, you can tell all that. I mean, you can tell all-l that just by looking at that tree. Marvelous. Amazing. A-*maz*-z-zing!

ALICE: No more, George. Your games don't work an-ny more.

GEORGE: Because you know what I mean by what I do? Because you know what I mean by what I say?

ALICE: From A to Z. A to Z.

GEORGE: Impressive — that is impressive. From *A* to *Z*.

[Sitting comfortably in sofa.] But, uh, you're sure . . . you're quite sure of that?

ALICE: Hah. Still, still playing games.

GEORGE: I, *I've* given them up — because you, you are, Alice.

ALICE: What do you mean by that?

GEORGE: *[Breaking out in laughter.]* Hah-h! Hah-h-h-h! You said you knew what I meant!

ALICE: I do know, oh, I do know.

GEORGE: Oh, Alice-ce! Hah-h-h-h! I'd like to — hah-h — You know, Alice . . . All right, all right, I'm, I'm-m going to tell you. By God, Alice, I am, I am. Some day I'm going to tell you why I really, really — why I really bought that tree — that blue spruce. I am going to tell you . . . some day. Why and how and under what circumstances I got that blue spruce.

ALICE: I don't for one moment doubt it. I'm sure you will.

GEORGE: Careful, be care-ful, Alice. I'm really going to tell you. And when I do . . . you . . . won't . . . like it. You're not going to like it.

ALICE: Ah-h-h-h . . .

GEORGE: It's going to hurt your pride, Alice. Your rich sensitivity and all that. Because you haven't the faintest . . . not-t the faintest . . . the remotest, faintest — The way things happen, the way they actually happen, and why they happen. And what people mean by what they say. That's not a game for you.

ALICE: What do you mean by that?

GEORGE: Al-lice . . . You said you knew-w. *[Stopping her as she begins to form the same question in stubborn spite.]*

Ah-h-h . . . Ah-H-H . . . Don't . . . don't say it again. Don't.
Either of us, either of us, ever, *ever.*
ALICE: *[Suddenly pulling the rug from under his smugness.]*
What makes you think that tree is going to stay there?
That-t tree?
GEORGE: ????
ALICE: There'll be no tree out there. Not out there.
GEORGE: Hello. Come again. What??
ALICE: I don't want any tree out there — I said no-o tree.
GEORGE: What do you mean by that?
ALICE: *[Her turn to be amused.]* Oh-h-h. . .?
GEORGE: *[Obdurate.]* I said what do you mean by that?
ALICE: I heard you, I heard you, George. And maybe,
maybe some day I'll tell you. Maybe some day I will. But
you won't like it. No, you won't. It's going to hurt your
pride, your nimble mind, your famous, famous sixth sense,
your unruffled charm, and all that. All that, George. But,
still, maybe, some day, who knows — I may tell you why I
don't want a tree out there — *any* tree *out there.* Ah-h, you're
surprised. You're surprised. Well, some day, maybe, I'll
tell you what I mean by that.
GEORGE: *[Calling a truce — with patent admiration.]* You
give as good as you get, don't you, Alice?
ALICE: Do you know what you mean by that, George?
GEORGE: *[Pulling his hair in mock pain.]* Stop it, Alice!
Stop it! Stop it! If I ever hear that again! Again! Again!
Again-n! *[A pause. Suddenly ALLEN bounces in from the
patio.]*
ALLEN: Whatta you mean by that? Hey, Alice, George!?
We had to show that tree guy how to get here?
CHARLOTTE: *[Striding in from front door.]* Hey, George,

Alice!? Your tree man was lost! What do you mean by that!?

CHARLOTTE and ALLEN: Whatta you mean by that!?

[GEORGE and ALICE register the appropriate gamut of surprise and amusement.]

ALICE and GEORGE: Whatta you mean by that!? *[Collective laughter as they all look out at the tree, really the audience, and the question could be to the audience.]*

CURTAIN